ICT AND PRIMARY
MATHEMATICS

Learning and Teaching with Information and Communications Technology

Series editors: Tony Adams and Sue Brindley

The role of ICT in the curriculum is much more than simply a passing trend. It provides a real opportunity for teachers of all phases and subjects to rethink fundamental pedagogical issues alongside the approaches to learning that pupils need to apply in classrooms. In this way it foregrounds the way in which teachers can match in school the opportunities for learning provided in home and community. The series in firmly rooted in practice and also explores the theoretical underpinning of the ways in which curriculum content and skills can be developed by the effective integration of ICT in schooling. It addresses the educational needs of the early years, the primary phase and secondary subject areas. The books are appropriate for pre-service teacher training and continuing professional development as well as for those pursuing higher degrees in education.

Published and forthcoming titles:

R. Barton (ed.): *Learning and Teaching Science with ICT*
Florian and Hegarty (eds): *ICT and Special Educational Needs*
A. Loveless and B. Dore (eds): *ICT in the Primary School*
M. Monteith (ed.): *Teaching Primary Literacy with ICT*
J. Way and T. Beardon (eds): *ICT and Primary Mathematics*

ICT AND PRIMARY MATHEMATICS

Edited by
Jenni Way and Toni Beardon

Open University Press
Maidenhead · Philadelphia

Open University Press
McGraw-Hill Education
Shoppenhangers Road
Maidenhead
Berkshire
England
SL6 2QL

email: enquiries@openup.co.uk
world wide web: www.openup.co.uk

and
325 Chestnut Street
Philadelphia, PA 19106, USA

First Published 2003

A catalogue record of this book is available from the British Library

ISBN 0 335 21030 9 (pb)   0 335 21031 7 (hb)

Library of Congress Cataloging-in-Publication Data
Way, Jenni (Jennifer Anne), 1956–
    ICT and primary mathematics / Jenni Way and Toni Beardon.
        p. cm. – (Learning and teaching with ICT)
    Includes bibliographical references and index.
    ISBN 0–335–21031–7 – ISBN 0–335–21030–9 (pbk.)
    1. Mathematics–Computer-assisted instruction. 2. Mathematics–Study and teaching (Primary)–Data processing. 3. Educational technology. I. Beardon, Toni (Leonora Antoinette), 1940– II. Title. III. Series.

QA20.C65 W39 2003
372.7′044 – dc21

Typeset by RefineCatch Limited, Bungay, Suffolk
Printed in Great Britain by Bell and Bain, Glasgow

CONTENTS

LIST OF CONTRIBUTORS

Toni Beardon, University of Cambridge. After a long career in secondary mathematics teaching and teacher education with Cambridge University, Toni founded the NRICH Online Mathematics Club and other related projects. Her research interests include peer assisted learning and the impact of the Internet on learning and teaching mathematics. In 2002, Toni was awarded an OBE for services to mathematics education.

Merilyn Buchanan, California State University. Merilyn has taught across all age groups from kindergarten to college in Britain and the USA. She taught for 12 years as a demonstration teacher and education lecturer at the University of California, Los Angeles, worked for a year as the NRICH Primary Mathematics Coordinator for the Royal Institution and the University of Cambridge, and then returned to a post at California State University.

Ruth Forrester, University of Edinburgh. Ruth, an experienced teacher, works with the Edinburgh Centre for Mathematical Education, University of Edinburgh, as a research development officer with a particular interest in supporting teachers in their explorations of using calculators with their classes.

Ronnie Goldstein, Open University. Ronnie has an extensive background in mathematics education in secondary schools, universities and with BECTA. He has designed and produced a wide range of learning materials and computer-based resources including Logo MicroWorlds programs, SMILE programs and dynamic geometry packs. He is also known for his active involvement in The Association for Teachers in Mathematics and as editor of the *Micromath* journal (1989–94).

Pat Perks, University of Birmingham. Pat comes from a background in secondary mathematics teaching and has also worked with many primary schools in the role of an advisory teacher. A major focus of her recent work has been the use of the calculator and ICT in primary mathematics.

David Pratt, University of Warwick. After a 15-year teaching career, David moved into mathematics education lecturing in primary and secondary courses. Since joining the University of Warwick his research has focused on the relationship between virtual tools and the emergence of mathematical knowledge. He is currently involved in the Playground Project, based at the Institute of Education, University of London, in which young children construct and modify video-type games.

Stephanie Prestage, University of Birmingham. Stephanie has broad experience in education, having taught mathematics in secondary schools, worked on major primary school curriculum projects, tutored on secondary mathematics education courses and taught Masters level ICT modules for primary mathematics. Her recent interest has been in the development of algebra in Years 5 and 6.

Jenni Way, University of Western Sydney. Jenni has taught in primary schools in Australia. She spent two and a half years with the Cambridge University School of Education developing the NRICH Prime website and with the Royal Institution helping to set up school lectures and a network of primary masterclasses around the UK. Jenni has now returned to her mathematics education lecturing position in Sydney.

John Vincent, Melbourne Grammar School. John has extensive teaching experience and is currently working at Melbourne Grammar School, where he is Coordinator of Information and Learning Technologies. He is currently engaged in a PhD study involving children's learning styles and their interaction with computer software.

SERIES EDITORS' PREFACE

Jenni Way and Toni Beardon are known nationally and internationally for their work on mathematics, Toni Beardon as instigator and Project Director of NRICH, a website devoted to mathematically gifted and talented students worldwide and Jenni Way as NRICH Primary Project Coordinator. We are delighted therefore to have their volume *ICT and Primary Mathematics* as part of our series on teaching with ICT. At the heart of their success lies not only their extensive and undoubted subject knowledge but also a central tenet about the teaching and learning of mathematics: that mathematics should be enjoyed. ICT is an integral part of bringing about that enjoyment, and thereby extending understanding.

ICT can also be said to owe a particular debt to mathematics: it is clearly a truism that the beginnings of computing originated in mathematics.

It is generally accepted that the founder of modern computing was Charles Babbage with his development of the Difference Engine, essentially an elaborate calculating machine that could operate on the basis of a series of different programmable calculating registers. Much more revolutionary was Babbage's concept of the Analytical Engine where efficiency and economy was to be achieved by the separation of the functions of storage and arithmetic calculation. Here, in fact, were the beginnings of the modern computer. Hofstadter in *GODEL, ESCHER, BACH* (Penguin Books, 1979) argued that Babbage was 'profoundly aware that, with the invention of the Analytical Engine, mankind was flirting with mechanical intelligence'. Like Alan Turing's 'universal machine', the Analytical Engine was never constructed but the two concepts have really combined to inform what is meant by ICT today in both society and education.

In the work undertaken on school mathematics teaching through NRICH http://www.nrich.maths.org.uk, Way and Beardon have brought together ideas pioneered by Babbage and Turing. To this we must add the work of another major pioneer of computers in education, Seymour Papert, whose *Mindstorms: Children, Computers and Powerful Ideas* (Harvester Press, 1980) and even more importantly, *The Children's Machine* (Basic Books, 1993), recognized that computers in education were essentially a means of empowerment, giving school pupils control over their own learning environment.

Although Papert's development of LOGO was essentially concerned with mathematics teaching in the first instance, the concrete representation of the mathematical processes involved through the use of a mechanical object (the 'turtle') made what Papert called 'powerful ideas' accessible to primary (elementary) school students. This volume provides teachers with insights into how other teachers and researchers have discovered ways to create powerful learning experiences for children. Each chapter helps the reader to understand why certain teaching approaches with technology are more effective than others, as well as providing many practical ideas for activities and projects for children with various ability levels and learning styles.

Way and Beardon demonstrate that ICT has a plurality of functions: calculators and computers can be used as tools in mathematics to perform routine processes or to explore mathematical ideas; graphic and programmable calculators, and computers with open-ended software can also immerse children in exciting, creative and productive learning environments; and the Internet allows children to venture into the enormous world of mathematics beyond the classroom.

Although its main audience is likely to be mathematics coordinators in the primary school, we feel that teachers of other subjects, like ourselves, can benefit from its insights into education in the widest sense of the word.

We commend it as a scholarly and humane approach to its subject that worthily builds on its theoretical predecessors in the field of mathematical education and computing theory.

Anthony Adams & Sue Brindley

PREFACE

Even after more than 20 years of computers and calculators in classrooms, technology is still not fully integrated into mathematics teaching in many schools. Computers, the various types of calculator, generic applications including spreadsheets, databases, LOGO programming and dynamic geometry software, a wide range of learning 'packages' and now the Internet, all have the potential to be powerful tools for enhancing children's learning. This book draws on the experience and research of teachers and educators to give teachers practical ideas that they can implement in their own classrooms and insight into the possibilities for exciting outcomes from children's interaction with technology. As teachers, we need to understand how the features of calculators, computers and the Internet can support the way we choose to teach and how they relate to the learning styles of children and to the mathematical concepts and skills they need to learn.

This book discusses 'what to do', 'how to do' and 'why you would want to do' mathematics with technology, suggesting ideas that any teacher can adopt with whatever scant technology is available as well as some new ideas from research with very new technology and software. There are insights into the ways in which teachers can use calculators and computers to support their own mathematics learning and teaching, to encourage mathematical thinking and to enhance children's learning. The technologies now available provide the tools to access new information, to explore ideas in powerful ways and to make use of resources from around the world. The book provides a mixture of 'ideas to use today' and a taste of the exciting teaching and learning experiences that lie ahead for those willing to 'have a go'.

Toni Beardon

1

DIGITAL TECHNOLOGIES + MATHEMATICS EDUCATION = POWERFUL LEARNING ENVIRONMENTS

Jenni Way and Toni Beardon

Digital technologies

The aim of this book is to provide teachers and educators with sufficient evidence to convince them that the permeation of society by digital technologies has brought education to a point where teachers have an overpowering responsibility to incorporate these technologies effectively into their teaching. The authors enthusiastically share their experiences, discoveries and convictions in an effort to inspire and support other teachers to realize the importance of such technologies in mathematics education and in children's lifelong learning.

Digital technologies are devices that store, process and communicate information in a coded form. The coding system is binary – that is, it only uses two digits, 0 and 1. Each of these binary digits is called a 'bit' and bits are usually counted in groups of eight, known as 'bytes'. Images as well as text can be coded, or 'bitmapped', and then each 'bit' is known as a pixel (picture element). Central to digital technology are the computer and the Internet, though there is an increasing range of *converging technologies* that can exchange data with computers, such as graphic calculators, data loggers, cameras, handheld organizers, mobile phones and interactive whiteboards.

Mathematics education

The mathematics education community is engaged in a constant quest to find out how children best learn mathematics. Mathematics is an enormous and constantly expanding network of interrelated facts and ideas. Just as complicated are the fields of cognitive development and the psychology of learning. A large proportion of teachers these days try to base much of their teaching practice on constructivist ideas – that is, on the belief that the teacher's role is to create opportunities for children to build their own understandings of concepts. If only we could discover precisely how the child best learns mathematics then we could work out exactly how to teach the child the subject in the most effective way. Many would say that this is an impossible dream. We can never achieve ultimate professional enlightenment, not only because every child and every teacher is different, but because the social and cultural contexts keep changing. Schools are forced to be responsive to changes in social, political and economic situations, and the impact of advances in science and technology cannot be underestimated. How can teachers excel at the 'game' when the playing field is different every time we run onto it and the 'governing body' has changed the rules again? We think we have mastered substantial and worthy teaching methodologies and then we are told they are outdated, or need changing in the light of new research findings. Teachers react to pressures for change in their teaching methods with responses across the whole spectrum ranging from denial and refusal to an enthusiastic reception of new ideas.

Digital technologies + mathematics education

So what does this talk of teaching methodology have to do with technologies in mathematics education? Aren't the machines just resources, tools to be used within mathematics lessons? Teachers have now been struggling for many years to integrate calculators and computers effectively into their day-to-day teaching, but for most it just has not been successful. Why not? Could it be because they have been trying to 'add on' computer resources to established patterns of teaching? Does it really make sense to try to teach children using methods grounded in the past, in the context of the present, to prepare them for the future? Is there another way in which we should be viewing the role of digital technologies?

Digital technologies, in particular the Internet, can be seen as catalysts for a paradigm shift. Since printed material and books became readily accessible, education has experienced a gradual shift away from the idea that its success relies on the student's capacity to memorize and accurately recall large amounts of information. Instead, greater emphasis has been placed on developing research and problem-solving skills. In recent years, with emerging information and communication technologies (ICTs), the pressure has rapidly mounted to shift our views on effective teaching and learning even further. (Emphasis is now placed on equipping students with effective inquiry skills, including the ability to find and process new ⅄ information using digital technologies.) Many educators are now seeing digital technologies, with their interconnectedness, as *environments*, rather than just *tools*, for learning and teaching. The difference between these two perspectives is significant, the former requiring a fundamental change in teaching practice for many teachers.

Technical skills versus thinking skills

The emphasis in schools is increasingly on *learning how to learn*, rather than just acquiring specific technical skills that keep changing anyway. Children must have the ability to cope with change and accept innovation. Their ICT skills need to be integrated with their analytical abilities, creative capacity, cooperative work skills, problem-solving strategies and communication skills. The current trends in further education and workplace environments require computer literacy skills, including Internet usage, of a relatively high order. This means students need to develop good technical skills, literacy and numeracy, an awareness of their own thinking and problem-solving strategies (metacognition) and, most importantly, self-management skills. Not only do children need to develop effective search skills to locate likely information for their use, but they must also develop the ability to be critical in their choices. These are also new skills for teachers.

The world online

Statistics gathered on Internet usage are diverse, but all sources forecast continued rapid growth. Despite many surveys, published figures on Internet usage are only estimates. For example, NUA Internet Surveys gives the figure of 605.6 million Internet users worldwide in September 2002 (just under 10 per cent of the world's population). However, in March 1999, Datamonitor PLC estimated only 150 million users worldwide and predicted an increase to 300 million by the year 2005. In addition, so rapid is the growth of the Internet, that statistics are out of date as soon as they are published. (This inevitably makes the Internet the best source of such information because of the speed in which current information can be made available to the public through this medium.) Nevertheless the figures presented in Table 1.1 will give the reader a sense of the scale and speed of the development of the Internet and also an

Table 1.1   Estimated number of people using the Internet

Region	Millions of users
Africa	6.31
Asia/Pacific	187.24
Europe	190.91
Middle East	5.12
Canada & USA	182.67
Latin America	33.35
World total	**605.60**

Source: NAU Internet Surveys, September 2002

Table 1.2   Internet usage in countries where English is the dominant language

Country	Millions of Internet users	Percentage of population
Ireland	1.30	33.67
UK	34.00	56.88
Australia	10.63	54.38
New Zealand	1.95	49.9
USA	165.75	59.1
Canada	16.99	53.26

Source: NUA Internet Surveys, February/May 2002

indication of the trends in its usage. As would be expected, the wealthier and more industrially developed regions of the world have more people connected to and using the Internet. Higher figures in Internet usage are also linked with political orientations towards promoting open dissemination of information. Table 1.1 lists the estimated number of users of the Internet in the six major regions of the world in September 2002. Canada and the USA, Europe and Asia/Pacific are each approaching 200 million users. A very large gap lies between these figures and the numbers given for Africa, the Middle East and Latin America.

A clearer picture of the extent to which Internet usage has permeated society in various regions or countries can be gained through looking at figures that indicate the proportion of the population online rather than the raw number of users. For example, although there were 10.63 million users in Australia in February–May 2002 and only 1.95 million in New Zealand, these figures represent 54.38 per cent and 49.9 per cent of the respective populations (see Table 1.2). These proportions suggest that Internet usage is integrated into these societies to a similar extent, despite the difference of about 8 million users.

These figures just give a snapshot of the situation at a particular point in time. They do not indicate growth trends.

Students minus Internet equals the digital divide

Around the world, nations have struggled to reduce the gap between educationally disadvantaged people and those with full access to education – with some degree of success. However, with the emergence of Internet technology a new gap has opened up: the digital divide.

Here is some sobering information from UNICEF (1999): about one sixth of the global population is illiterate (855 million), with two thirds of these being women. Even if they had access to the technology, the Internet is closed to those who can't read. UNICEF estimates that 21 per cent of primary-age children in the world (130 million) do not have access to basic education. Another way of looking at it is that for every person that has Internet access, five people cannot read. In developed countries, while our difficulties are not as daunting as those faced by less fortunate populations, access to digital technologies is not uniform.

Consider the implications of the following statement that formed part of the conclusions drawn from a nationwide study done in Australia (DETYA 1999): 'Although all schools have had computers for many years and Internet connection for several years, there is an overall tendency for students to acquire their *advanced* technology skills at home rather than at school'. This implies that the children are doing something with the technologies at home that they not doing at school. Is it just a matter of greater access time at home? Or is it perhaps that the children have greater freedom to explore, experiment and be creative at home than in a restrictive classroom environment? And what of the children who do not have computer access at home – where will they gain their advanced skills? Are schools somehow increasing the digital divide rather than decreasing it? It appears that it isn't enough just to have the technologies available – it is how the technologies are *used* that makes the difference to the quality of learning.

Conclusion

The characteristics of digital technology provide potentially powerful learning tools, but in schools it's the teacher who creates the learning environment that either unleashes this potential or inhibits it. Each chapter of this book provides examples of ways in which a teacher can create learning environments likely to maximize the educational benefits of using digital technologies. These learning environments exist, at least partially, within the technologies themselves.

References

DETYA (Department of Education, Training and Youth Affairs) (1999) *Real Time: Computers, Change and Schooling.* www.detya.gov.au/schools/publications/ index.htm

Websites

Australian Bureau of Statistics: www.abs.gov.au
DataMonitor PLC: www.media.awareness.ca.eng/issues/stats/usenet.htm
NUA Surveys: www.nua.ie/surveys/index.cgi
UNICEF: www.unicef.org/sowc99rite.htm

2

IT'S NOT CALCULATORS
BUT HOW THEY'RE
USED . . .

Ruth Forrester

Why use calculators?

It serves no useful purpose to give a child a calculator and a page of traditional calculations such as 2 + 8 or 26 – 14. In contrast, giving that child a calculator and asking how many different calculations can be found with the answer 10 has quite a different effect. The learner may find 2 + 8, 3 + 7, 4 + 6 . . . (a pattern); 11 – 1, 12 – 2, 13 – 3 . . . (another pattern). There are opportunities to explore multiplication and division, fractions and negative numbers. Such open-ended tasks help children to develop a feel for number by exploring number properties for themselves. Learners can make and test conjectures and are able to correct their misunderstandings experientially. Pupils can work at a variety of different levels and all experience success. There is a clear positive effect on motivation.

Groups of teachers working with researchers (led by Dr John Searl) at the Edinburgh Centre for Mathematical Education have been investigating the possibilities of calculator use in the classroom. One teacher's comment perhaps sums up the findings: 'It is not calculators, but how they are used that is important'.

This chapter contains descriptions of a variety of calculator activities found by this group to work well in their classrooms as they teach in their different ways (the calculators are, however, just a tool – the focus is on learning mathematics). At the same time, more general consideration is given to the opportunities offered by calculator use.

Many of the ideas require only basic calculators, but graphic calculators open up more possibilities, particularly for shape and graph work. A class set of graphic calculators allows each pupil to have a simple 'mini-computer' at their own desk, available when required without a trip to the school computer suite. The screen of a graphic calculator can be easily shown to the whole class using an overhead projector and view screen. Programs running simple games and also data lists can be passed from one machine to another or downloaded from the computer. Data (e.g. sound measurements) can be collected directly by probe and fed automatically into the calculator.

Number

Learning number facts

Calculators can be used effectively to provide lots of repeated practice of number facts. Here the key is to find an activity where the learner is given the answer and has to find the question. For example, the snake race is a great favourite. Figure 2.1 shows a version devised by two 10-year-olds.

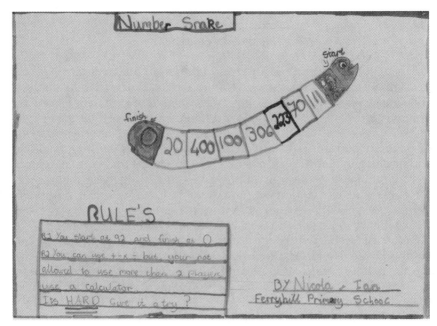

Figure 2.1 The snake race

Start at the head and key '92' into the calculator. Add, subtract, multiply or divide by something to make the calculator show the next number, 111. If the pupil misses and gets, say, 110, they carry on with another operation (+1) to get 111. Continue down the snake in the same way to finish with the tail number, 0. Pupils can time themselves or race against a partner.

The snake's numbers can be chosen to give practice in particular facts (e.g. limited to addition or subtraction facts under 20), and in the context of a game pupils are happy to repeat the exercise several times in order to improve their time. Feedback is instant. There is no need to wait for the teacher to come along with a red pen – pupils correct their mistakes straight away. This type of activity helps to build confidence as mistakes can be made in private and corrected. Just having a calculator in the hand can encourage an anxious pupil to have a go, even though it isn't giving them the answers!

Children will often try much harder examples when using calculators, and are particularly interested in exploring large numbers. For example, a group of 6- and 7-year-olds were playing 'Can you get a bull's eye?' (see Figure 2.2). They had to find what to add or subtract to the start number to hit the target. The teacher's examples all used numbers under 20, but when asked to make some more for each other, one pair introduced numbers involving hundreds.

'Connect Four' (see Figure 2.3) is another very adaptable game, which is good for practising number facts. Different operations and numbers can be used to adapt this game as appropriate. Multiplication of decimals, for example, can make this game very challenging, even for adults! It then

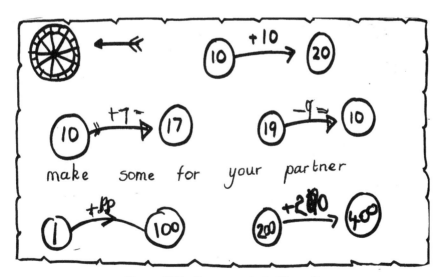

Figure 2.2   Can you get a bull's eye?

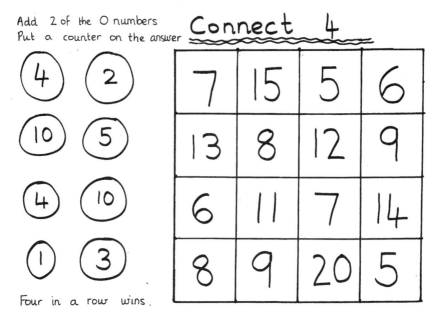

Figure 2.3 Connect Four

becomes a game that encourages estimation rather than recall of number bonds.

Developing number sense

Estimation skills are very important. With calculator use, pupils need to know when an answer makes sense and when it doesn't. It is important that they do not accept the answer shown on the calculator without question. Such number sense can only be developed with practice and calculator games are particularly effective in this context. 'The decimals game' is a good example. Played in pairs, one player chooses a target number and the other a starting number. Players take turns to choose a number to multiply by so that the target is reached. The winner is the first to get within 1 of the target number. Pupils enthusiastically play this game over and over again. Here, for example, Koo played against Eddie (see Figure 2.4):

Koo set the target, 100.
Eddie started with 4.
Koo multiplied by 50, too much.
Eddie multiplied by 2.5, getting larger.
Koo realized he had to multiply by a number less than one.
Eddie followed suit, giving Koo an easy finish.

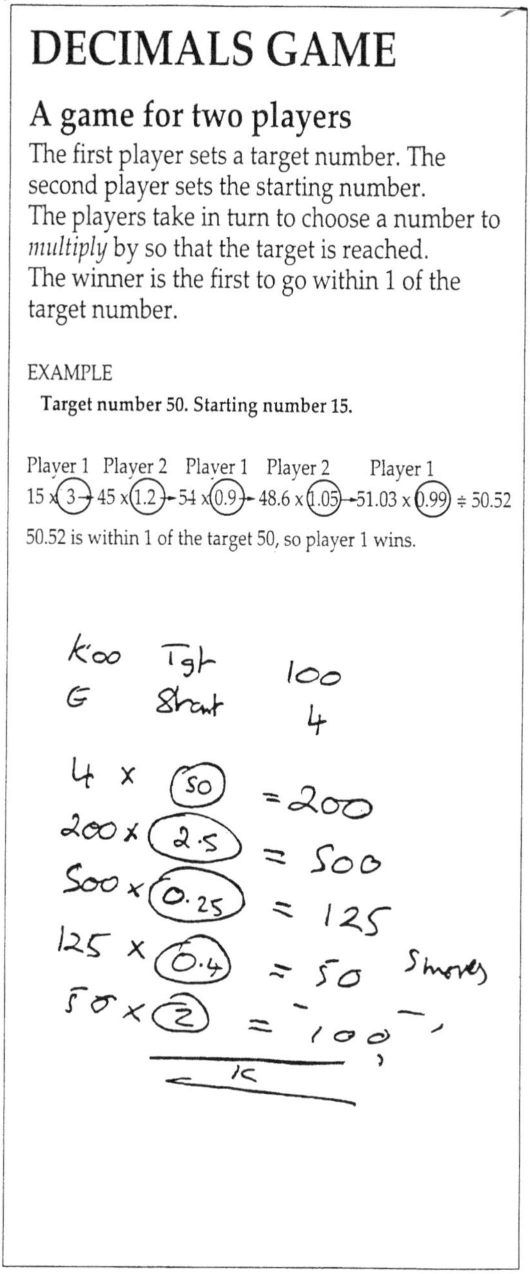

DECIMALS GAME

A game for two players

The first player sets a target number. The
second player sets the starting number.
The players take in turn to choose a number to
multiply by so that the target is reached.
The winner is the first to go within 1 of the
target number.

EXAMPLE

Target number 50. Starting number 15.

Player 1 Player 2   Player 1   Player 2   Player 1
15 x ③→ 45 x ⑴.2→ 54 x ⑴.9→ 48.6 x ⑴.05→51.03 x ⑴.99 ÷ 50.52

50.52 is within 1 of the target 50, so player 1 wins.

K'00   Tgt   100
G   Start   4

4 x ㊿ = 200
200 x ②.5 = 500
500 x ⓪.25 = 125
125 x ⓪.4 = 50   5 moves
50 x ② = ⁻100⁻
⎯⎯⎯⎯⎯⎯⎯
← 1<

Figure 2.4   The decimals game

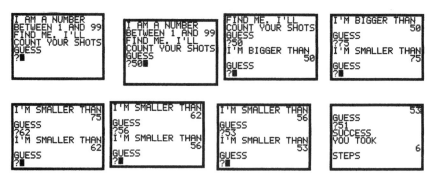

Figure 2.5 Eight stages in a 'Find me' game on a graphic calculator

The game provides the motivation for lots of practice, while the calculator provides speedy feedback after every guess. The estimation skills of the pupils can be seen to improve rapidly in this situation.

Graphic calculators can be programmed to run simple games. 'Find me' helps to develop a feel for number as well as encouraging pupils to seek an efficient strategy to find the required number in as few steps as possible. The calculator prompts 'I am a number between 1 and 99. Find me. I'll count your shots. Guess?' and the pupil must respond by inputting a number (e.g. 50). The calculator replies with a message such as 'I'm bigger than 50. Guess?' and the process continues until the correct number is input. Pupils devise various methods for finding the number quickly, such as guessing 10, 20, 30, 40 and so on until they get close, or using 'interval halving' (see Figure 2.5). They can discuss their strategies and use the game to test out and compare the alternatives.

Understanding averages

'Average X' is a game suitable for a group of 11- or 12-year-olds, that also builds estimation skills. Five pupils each choose a number between 0 and 100 and a sixth chooses a target number. Pupils use calculators to work out the average of the sets of (originally five) numbers. Class members are invited to suggest numbers to add to the (growing) set of data so that the average hits the target (within one unit). This game appeared in *Calculators in the Secondary School* (Graham *et al.* 1986).

Pupils become very involved in such games. One teacher described how a group of pupils normally indifferent to mathematics played 'Average X' and enthusiastically moved towards the target. When one pupil suggested a number that would obviously take the average in the wrong direction, his disgruntled friend threw a pencil at him! Pupils naturally seek for efficient ways to calculate the new average when one extra number is added to the set, and they gain a dynamic understanding of the concept of an average.

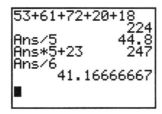

Figure 2.6 Part of a game of 'Average X' played on a graphic calculator

The game can be played using basic calculators, but graphic calculators, if available, offer advantages. The steps involved in calculating a new average can be seen on the larger screen, so a pupil can look back at this when explaining (vocalizing) how the calculation was done (see Figure 2.6). Notice the use of 'Ans', which allows the previous answer to be used in the next step of the calculation.

Exploring number patterns

On graphic calculators, the same calculation can be quickly repeated over and over again, allowing exploration of number patterns. For example, repeated addition of 9 gives rise to the 9 times table (see Figure 2.7), and the addition of the digits becomes more interesting later in the sequence as the numbers become larger . . .

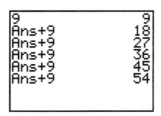

Figure 2.7 Exploring number patters: repeated addition of 9 produces the 9 times table

Children are keen to explore multiplication tables they don't know. Alannah wrote the 15 times table on a coloured strip and added the comment: 'I have noticed that all the last numbers go 5, 0, 5, 0 . . . and all the first numbers go funny' (see Figure 2.8).

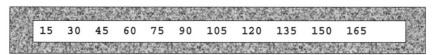

Figure 2.8 Alannah's 15 times table

Order of operations

'Four 4s' is another activity where a graphic calculator is an advantage. Pupils are asked which totals up to 10 can be made with 4, 4, 4, 4 by inserting $+ - \times$ or $\div$ between the fours. Children soon find some 'funny answers'. Should $4 + 4 \div 4 + 4$ come to 9? Why not 6? The calculator is the perfect tool to investigate the order of operations. The large screen allows groups of calculations to be compared and expressions can be edited to change the order or add brackets (Forrester and Searl 2000).

More number concepts

A very effective open-ended activity for building number concepts comes from the CAN (Calculator Aware Number) project (Shuard *et al.* 1991). Pick a number and write it in the centre of a square. Find four corner numbers, that add to give the centre number. This is a tremendously rich activity that can be used at many levels. Figure 2.9 shows some squares selected from those produced by a 9-year-old girl. She started with some simple examples but was soon keen to try much larger numbers. She was delighted with her system for easily doing examples involving thousands. The teacher suggested trying to find four equal corner numbers. She found this hard at first, using trial and error, but then realized she could divide by four! Then she found a strange one: 2.75. The teacher used the opportunity to discuss what this might mean and they used plastic money to help make sense of the answer.

This deceptively simple activity provides opportunities for pupils to build concepts of addition, place value, estimation, division, the connection between addition and multiplication, and decimals. The activity can be varied by using other shapes instead of squares. Triangles, for example, can lead to consideration of the meaning of the recurring decimal 0.333.

Understanding place value

A graphic calculator can help to promote understanding of the concept of place value. The game of 'Space Invaders' is very effective, whereby the children enter a number into the calculator (e.g. 857) and the digits represent the aliens who then have to be 'shot down' by subtracting to zero (see Figure 2.10). Pupils who try to shoot down the 5 by simply subtracting 5 can see their mistake immediately and quickly discover for themselves that they need to subtract 50. Other versions of this game include use of decimals, shooting down by adding (e.g. $837 + 70 = 907$ to shoot down the alien 3) or moving to the unit's position before shooting (e.g. $837 \div 10 = 83.7, 83.7 - 3 = 80.7$ to shoot down the 3).

Place value is central to the understanding of number but not easy to teach. Tricks with zeros and points, shown by a teacher, may not make the

Jean (primary 5 - age 9)   Curriehill Primary School

Figure 2.9   Number squares

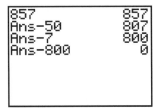

Figure 2.10 'Space Invaders'

concept clear to pupils. Games like space invaders can be of help because they give pupils the time and motivation to 'suss out' the ideas for themselves, so gaining a deeper understanding of the concept.

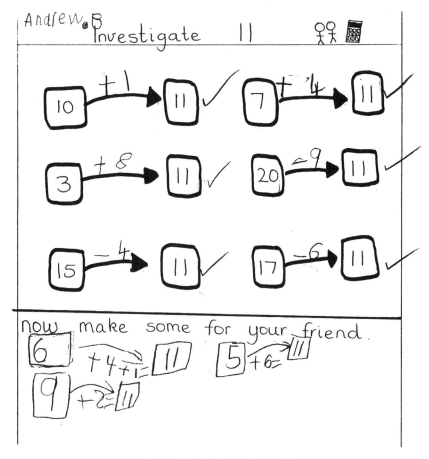

Figure 2.11 'Investigate 11'

Algebraic concepts

Some types of number work can build ideas that lay the foundation for algebraic concepts. In the activity 'Investigate 11', for example, pupils are asked to find the missing operations and numbers (see Figure 2.11).

Activities involving the use of memories A, B, C, etc. on a graphic calculator can help pupils develop the idea of a variable that may take different numerical values. In the game shown in Figure 2.12, Player 1 stores a number in memory A and then clears the screen. Then Player 2 tries to work out the value of A by entering a calculation.

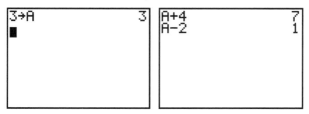

Figure 2.12   Using calculator memory to develop the idea of a variable ('A') that may take different numerical values

The 'loops activity' is useful for encouraging pupils to investigate the concept of inverse operations that is important for the later development of algebraic skills. Pupils must use + and −, or else × and ÷ to go round the loop and back to the start again. This activity can be more or less open-ended, depending on which boxes are left blank (see Figure 2.13).

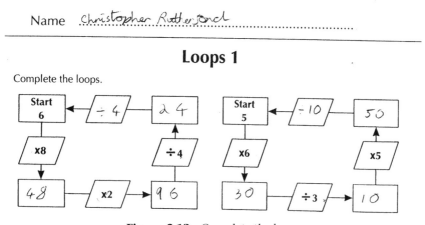

Figure 2.13   Complete the loops

Number in context

Using a calculator for money calculations can prompt children to think about place value. One teacher described a very fruitful discussion with her 9- and 10-year-old pupils, which started when she asked them to calculate £2.67 plus 35p on the calculator. Why did people get different answers? Another class ran the school tuckshop at morning break-times. They raised enough money to buy a laptop computer for the class! Deciding prices, stocktaking, selling and cashing up were all done by pupils (see Figure 2.14).

It is important that pupils practise the skills necessary to use the mathematics they know in context. In real life, numbers are often awkward. Calculators allow children to solve real-life problems without getting bogged down in arithmetic. Pupils are freed to look at the bigger picture and to concentrate on problem-solving strategies and the transfer between real life and its mathematical representation.

Hazel Howson

Tuck Shop

Item	Initial stock	unsold Pkts/cart	Pkts/cart sold	cost per PKT/cart	Selling price per PKT/cart	Total income	expenditure	Profit
Pineapple Juice	108	65	43	18p	25p	£10.75	£7.74	£3.01
apple Juice	81	70	11	18p	25p	£2.75	£1.98	£0.77
Orange Juice	54	46	8	18p	25p	£2.00	£1.44	£0.56
Raisins (1½oz)	60	38	22	17p	20p	£4.40	£3.74	£0.66
Flapjacks	72	41	31	19p	25p	£7.75	£5.89	£1.86
Grizzly bars	48	29	19	20p	25p	£4.75	£3.80	£0.95

Figure 2.14   The tuckshop

Shape

The use of calculators in the classroom is not restricted to number work, and can also help with pupils' understanding of shape.

Symmetry

'Clown' is a simple and effective activity that tackles symmetry. A program enables the graphic calculator to draw half of a clown's face, and pupils must draw in the other half. Those very keen to make their clown

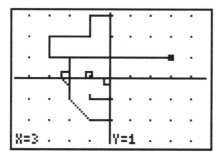

Figure 2.15 'Clown': learning symmetry

exactly symmetrical may use the coordinates displayed by the calculator while drawing. One pupil's attempt to ensure complete symmetry gave rise to a cross-eyed clown! A program is not essential here – one pupil can draw the first half of the face and their partner the other half (see Figure 2.15).

Coordinates

'Rhino' is one of the excellent MAD maths programs (see www.madmaths.net) which are helpful for early coordinate work. Pupils search for the rhino which is hidden somewhere on the 10 × 10 grid. Their chosen spot is labelled with a number indicating the number of 'grid-line units' away from the rhino – for example, three points are labelled 8, 8 and 18 in Figure 2.16 and the rhino is at (0, 9). Pupils compete to find the rhino in as few moves as possible and in the process have lots of practice using coordinates.

In the activity 'Shapes in the Dark', pupils work in pairs using one graphic calculator between them. The student without the calculator takes a card such as that shown in Figure 2.17. The cardholder then attempts to direct the other pupil to draw the same shape on the graphic calculator by giving them coordinates for the corners. For example, (1, 1), (6, 1), (6, 7) produces a right-angled triangle of the correct orientation, but since it is not an isosceles this student would score 1/2. Coordinates given as (0, 0),

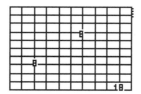

Figure 2.16 'Rhino'

Figure 2.17 'Shapes in the Dark'

(7, 0), (7, 7) would score 2/2. The pupils then swap places. Keen to score well, children quickly sort out the difference between (3, 5) and (5, 3) and the discussion involved in scoring each attempt leads to some very valuable development of mathematical language.

Angle

The graphic calculator can be used to practise estimation of angles. For example, the MAD maths game 'Airshot' invites pupils to shoot a clay pigeon by estimating the angle of fire. The idea is simple but effective. If they miss, pupils can see the line of fire on the screen and try again. The instant feedback and clay-pigeon shooting context encourages lots of practice.

Investigation

'Poly' is a program that gives rise to a variety of enriching mathematical activities for pupils. When a fraction is keyed in, such as $\frac{3}{7}$ or $\frac{3}{11}$ as shown in Figure 2.18, the calculator draws a star shape. Many pupils are fascinated by these shapes and if encouraged to explore their properties may make some interesting discoveries. For example, one group discovered:

- equivalent fractions give the same shape ($\frac{1}{2} = \frac{2}{4} = \ldots$);
- complementary fractions give the same shape ($\frac{3}{5} = \frac{2}{5}, \frac{5}{8} = \frac{3}{8}$);
- it is impossible to draw a six-pointed star;
- the denominator gives the number of vertices of the shape.

Each group in the class made a poster to show what they had discovered. Pupils from another class printed out their favourite designs to decorate the classroom.

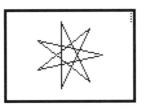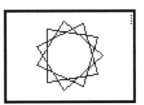

Figure 2.18 'Poly' shapes

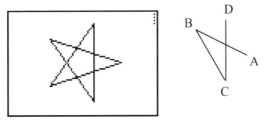

Figure 2.19 How a 'Poly' star is constructed

In fact, 'Poly' draws lines joining points on the circumference of an unseen circle. For example, when $\frac{2}{5}$ is entered, as in Figure 2.19, the program will start at A, go $\frac{2}{5}$ round the circle to B and join A and B with a straight line. It will then go $\frac{2}{5}$ round the circle to C and join B and C, and so on. This will continue until it comes back to A again. Pupils can be shown how the program draws the shape for $\frac{2}{5}$ by asking five of them to stand, evenly spaced, in a circle. The first person holds one end of a ball of string which is passed repeatedly to the person $\frac{2}{5}$ of the way round the circle.

Programming a computer to draw these stars in Logo provides a good follow-up activity and requires pupils to use their knowledge of angles and to see the drawings from a different perspective. They will need to work out the angle through which the turtle has to turn at each point in order to draw the star. As extension of this activity the most able programmers may be able to 'teach the computer' to draw wallpaper designs, repeating copies of the stars over and over again, as described in Chapter 5 (see p. 75).

This very rich activity can help pupils to appreciate links between art and mathematics, enable them to see that mathematical investigation does not always have just one right answer and encourage the development of mathematical language.

Data handling

Data-handling skills are increasingly important in society and this has been recognized with the increase in statistical content in school curricula. Graphic calculators offer a range of facilities for statistical calculations and graph plotting. Small amounts of data can be collected and analysed by hand, and this is a valuable experience for pupils. It is also important to be able to handle large data sets, to interpret information from displays and databases, and to handle real data in the way that statisticians do. Technology allows learners to deal with an amount of data large enough to make statistical analysis and plotting meaningful and helps them to make sense of the data. This promotes a deeper understanding of statistical concepts (such as the normal curve) gained through experience rather than at second hand by explanation.

Collection and representation of data

The following experiments undertaken by a class in Edinburgh were adapted from measurements and tests used by doctors in medical check-ups. Pupils gathered large amounts of data about class members and used graphic calculators to record and analyse the information. The data collected was:

- gender of pupil;
- eye colour;
- age in days;
- weekday of birthday this year;
- height;
- length of right foot;
- distance pupil can blow 1p across a desk;
- score when Blu-tack is dropped onto a target (0 – miss, to 8 – bullseye);
- length of time pupil can hold breath;
- volume of water drunk in one suck;
- number of steps (up and down) in 1 minute.

A 'stations' approach was used for the collection of data. One calculator, running the appropriate program, and the necessary equipment, were placed at each station. Pupils were divided into small groups and each group was given a record number. At each station the group carried out the experiment and members entered their own data onto their individual data sheet. Simple programs were used to help pupils key their results into the calculators without having to learn in detail how to operate lists on a graphic calculator. The programs also put the entries into order according to the pupils' record numbers.

The process of collecting the data offered considerable opportunity for collateral learning. Pupils were forced to consider the kinds of difficulties that may be faced when collecting real data. Rules had to be negotiated by the group so that results could be compared fairly (e.g. how far above the target should the Blu-tack be held before dropping? Can pupils have a practice shot? Did everyone take their shoes off to measure foot length? What about thick socks?). Issues of measurement became important to the pupils (e.g. which side of the coin should be measured to? How accurate should the measurement be – to the nearest centimetre or to 1 decimal place?).

After the data-gathering session, the lists of data were transferred from one calculator to another to compile a large database listing all the results together, ready for analysis.

For the second session, a whole-class approach was used. The teacher's calculator screen was shown on an overhead projector (OHP) and some pupils were able to work individually with the same data on their own calculators.

During the follow-up lesson, pupils were asked to sketch graphs before they were drawn on the calculator. They were asked to make suggestions for the window settings and to predict the shape of the graph in each case. These predictions were then discussed with the class as a whole and pupils' suggestions for maximum and minimum values on the axes were used to draw the graphs. This process had the advantage of providing a record of pupils' thinking as well as actively involving them in the lesson.

Pupils were clearly interested and involved in the lessons, and the technology played an important part in this. There was an audible 'ohh' when the first graph came up on the screen. Students were keen to suggest new graphs to try, and the facility to draw and redraw the same graphs with different scales was very effective – especially when pupils had different opinions about what the scales should be. The teachers involved were impressed by the way in which the lessons held the students' attention for the full hour. The fact that calculator use allowed the teacher to pace the lesson appropriately was significant here.

The fact that the pupils' own data was used also had a motivating effect. Pupils were very keen to look at the data in the lists and pick out particular people.

Pupil: That was me.
Pupil: I was on a Tuesday.

There was great interest in seeing the data referring to one particular boy (Gary), who is very tall. Jo-Ann picked out the point referring to Gary on her scatter graph, plotting height against foot length. Another pupil drew a separate bar for Gary on his histogram showing heights:

Pupil [*excited*]: That was Gary. 1.95! It had to be.

The class were also very anxious to pick out the data and position on the graph relating to another boy, Murray, who drank almost all the water in one suck:

Pupil [*excited*]: Miss Robertson, you said somebody drank all the water . . . somebody got 100mls.

When pupils were deciding on suitable axes for the graphs, they were able to refer back to their experience of making the measurements to help them choose sensible scales. For example, when suggesting suitable axes for the histogram of eye colour, one pupil suggested 0 to 15 because they thought there would be no more than half the class in each group. Another pupil chose 0 to 20 because they thought there would be a lot of brown eyes. They also used the data lists on the calculator.

Although corrections had been made to data wrongly entered, the learners were able to appreciate some of the difficulties of dealing with real data (e.g. missing data entered as zero and the effect of this on the resulting graphs).

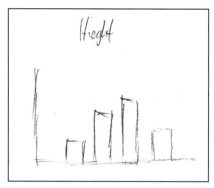

Figure 2.20 Arran and Heather's histogram for height

Andrew predicted a 'normal' curve but then modified his diagram to show more missing entries. The work on histograms helped many pupils to understand when they should expect a normal curve and when they should not. For example, Arran and Heather predicted normal curves when graphing the height of class members, the length of time they could hold their breath, the amount of water they could drink in one suck (see Figures 2.20 and 2.21). They both realized that the histogram showing which day of the week peoples' birthdays fall on would not have a normal shape since all the days are equally likely.

Having a lot of data and the facility to be able to draw a variety of graphs quickly helped the teacher to guide pupils' thinking about when and why a graph would take the form of a normal curve. Here is a sample discussion of predicted histogram results from steps data:

Pupil: It'll sort of go up and sort of at the top, it'll go down.
Teacher: Why do you think it will go up and then down again? Will they not all be the same?
Several Pupils [*firmly*]: No.
Pupil [*hesitating*]: There'll be quite a lot of people that'll get one thing, then it'll go off a bit, and there won't be very many people that get the other one.
Teacher: So there won't be very many people that get an awful lot. There won't be many 70s and 75s or 80s, right? There won't be very many 0s and 10s but is this what you're trying to say? There'll be an awful lot of something in the middle.
Pupil: Yes, yes.
Teacher: Let's graph it and see then.

A discussion of the day of the week histogram went like this:

Teacher: Can anybody predict for me, if I did a graph of what day of the week your birthdays were, what shape the graph would be?

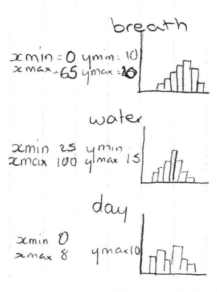

Figure 2.21 Arran and Heather's histograms for holding breath, sucking water and the day of the week on which a pupil's birthday fell. The latter is not a curve

Pupil: All scattered.
Pupil: All scattered, all up and down.

These activities helped pupils to understand when and why to expect a normal curve. The calculator use was significant in this, allowing the children to work with large amounts of data that they could make sense of – since they had gathered it themselves.

Applications to real problems

The statistical facilities of graphic calculators can also be used for the activity called 'How long is a piece of string?' Pupils are given a 10 cm length of string. They lay the string at random onto centimetre-squared paper and count how many times the string crosses a grid line. This is repeated and the data recorded (see Table 2.1). The same is done for 15,

Table 2.1 Data record from the activity 'How long is a piece of string?'

Length of string (cm)	Number of crossings
10	12
10	13
10	11
10	12

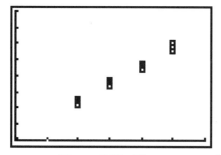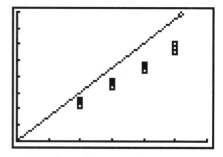

Figure 2.22   The scatter graphs resulting from the string data

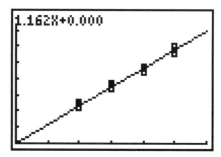

Figure 2.23   The line of 'best fit'

20 and 25cm lengths of string. Longer strings have more crossings. This data is entered in lists on a graphic calculator and a scatter graph is drawn (see Figure 2.22). On a TI73 calculator a line of 'best fit' can be drawn, as shown in Figure 2.23. The graph is traced to predict how many crossings would be expected for a 30cm length and the length of string with 48 crossings. Tracing is particularly useful as it helps pupils to see how each point on a graph makes a connection between two pieces of information.

Pupils are then given maps and work out the length of a main road by counting the number of grid lines crossed, and in this exercise they also have to take account of map scale. Over a series of three lessons, 11-year-olds who had never before used graphic calculators managed very successfully to enter the data into lists, draw scatter graphs and the line of best fit, and work with them to achieve very accurate estimates of road length. These were verified using mileage charts. These lessons were very successful, not only in terms of concept building but also in terms of attitudes to the learning of mathematics. The teacher felt that the pupils had benefited by learning to use the technology, but ultimately the calculator was just a tool – the focus was on the mathematics.

Automatic data collection

Data can be fed directly into the graphic calculator using a device such as the calculator-based laboratory (CBL) or the calculator-based ranger (CBR). The CBL can collect data such as temperature or light intensity, but the CBR is probably most useful in teaching mathematics. It detects the motion of a person or object and works in a way similar to a police speed gun, sending out rays which measure the distance from the CBR to the first object encountered. This data is fed back directly into the graphic calculator and can be graphed as appropriate. This means that a child can walk up and down the classroom in front of the CBR and a distance-time graph of their motion drawn as they walk. Pre-drawn distance time graphs can be very difficult to understand, but seeing the action take place at the same time as the graph is drawn is very effective in helping pupils to understand the dynamic aspect of the graph. Ten-year-old pupils using this equipment really enjoyed the experience and showed great gains in their understanding of graphs as well as of estimation of distance and time. They were able to work out for themselves, for example, how speed was related to the slope of the graph.

Conclusion

The graphic calculator is a useful tool that has much to offer in the primary classroom. Calculators can motivate pupils and give confidence to those anxious about mathematics. They give quick feedback without the necessity to ask the teacher and risk a big red cross. Ideas can be tested out privately using the calculator, which does not judge. Calculators can allow the teacher to vary a lesson, introducing an activity which will change the pace or type of action expected from pupils but continue the thinking, perhaps in a slightly different way.

Calculators can also be used to free children from the difficulties of paper and pencil calculation when the teacher wants to concentrate on the 'bigger picture', perhaps working on a real-life problem that may contain awkward numbers. They can be used to develop fluency in number, shape or graph work because they provide repeated practice and rapid experience of many examples. They provide opportunities to facilitate independent learning and give scope for open-ended exploration. Concepts that children build for themselves (rather than just hearing about them) are understood at a deeper level.

There are many good calculator activities that will enhance the learning experience for pupils. Different activities will be suitable for different classrooms, however the focus should be on the mathematics rather than the calculator. Some people have accused the calculator of making children lazy and replacing the need for them to think or remember number facts. In reality, the calculator is a tool that, if used in the right way, can support and encourage children's mathematical thinking.

References

Forrester, R. and Searl, J. (2000) *Uncle BODMAS and Old Friends, Mathematics Teaching MT173*, pp. 34–5. Lancashire: Association of Teachers of Mathematics.

Graham, G., Baker, J., Daniels, J. and Tyler, K. (1986) *Calculators in the Secondary School*. Cambridge: Cambridge University Press in association with the Open University.

Shuard, H., Walsh, A., Goodwin, J. and Worcester, V. (1991) *Calculators, Children, and Mathematics*. London: Simon & Shuster.

3
SPREADSHEETS WITH EVERYTHING

Pat Perks and Stephanie Prestage

Thinking about using a spreadsheet

Using information and communication technology (ICT) to enhance the teaching and learning of mathematics requires creativity on the part of the teacher. Essentially, ICT is a resource for doing mathematics and like other resources its use may change the way you teach a topic. You need to analyse the mathematics you are doing, or want to do, and decide how the technology might enhance your pupils' learning. Additionally, ICT can help with the organization of your teaching as computer files are easier to keep than paper. This chapter describes some of the ways a generic computer package – a spreadsheet – can be used for teaching mathematics.

Spreadsheets are computer progams not originally designed for use in schools. They are the tools of accountants and financial planners, but because they handle numbers well and draw statistical diagrams, they can be adapted in a variety of ways for use in the mathematics classroom.

The first thing to explore is the potential of a spreadsheet package for supporting the learning of mathematics. Microsoft Excel, readily available to schools, is used in the examples in this chapter. If you use different software, you will need to sort out the differences in syntax, but the

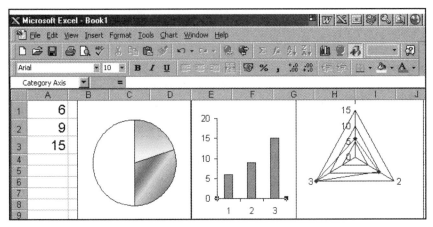

Figure 3.1 Alternative Excel diagrams to show the sequence 6, 9, 15

mathematics remains the same. Most spreadsheet packages offer large fonts, different fonts, formatting, diagrams, formulae and the opportunity to produce lots and lots of numbers. Generating random numbers using one of the given functions is a powerful alternative to flash cards. Patterns can be created with sequences of numbers or with colour, using the 'paint' facility (formatting with the brush symbol). Areas of the screen are easily copied to extend such patterns. Then there are lots and lots of different diagrams. Figure 3.1 shows some of the diagrams that are available to illustrate the sequence 6, 9, 15:

- a pie chart, which could be used to practise angle or proportion the attributes of a pie chart;
- a bar chart ('column graph' in Excel), which could be used for proportion and length;
- a web diagram – we are not sure how you would use that!

You can also use the scatter diagram facility, where two variables are connected, as if you were plotting coordinates, to produce shapes. In Figure 3.2, A2: B6 were highlighted to produce the diagram. You need to be careful to drag your axes into the size you want.

Having explored the possibilities of the software, you then have to make lots of other decisions based on normal planning for teaching, depending on whether you are:

- using one computer in the classroom, or a network;
- working with the whole class, with small groups or with individuals;
- constructing an activity for an oral/mental starter, other short activities introducing activities for the main part of the lesson or sharing findings in a plenary.

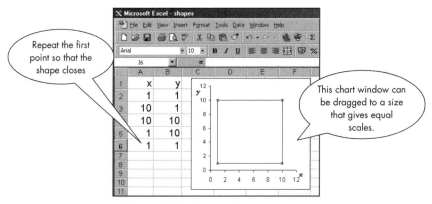

Figure 3.2 Scatter diagram square

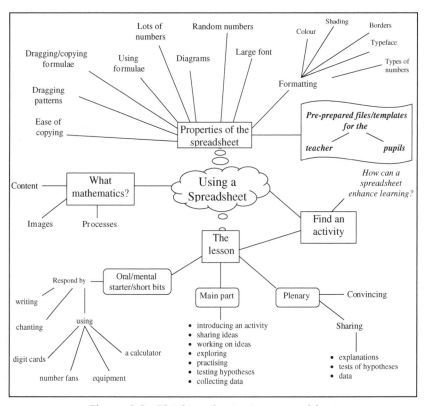

Figure 3.3 Thinking about using a spreadsheet

Finally, you have to create some activities! Figure 3.3 offers' a summary of, and expands upon, the ideas given so far. No doubt you could add to the diagram.

The next section offers some examples of how mathematics tasks can be enhanced by using spreadsheets. We will describe a range of activities using one computer with the class and in the network room when pupils can explore in pairs. There are ideas for oral sessions, main activities and the drawing together of pupils' explanations.

First ideas – nothing too technical

Here we will explore some of the immediate facilities of a spreadsheet in order to create some mathematics to demonstrate that you can use the software to great effect without too much know-how.

Large format

Most spreadsheets allow large fonts – you can enlarge a number so that it fills the monitor screen, and if the monitor is placed high enough this is sufficient for a whole class of children to see it – a sort of electronic flash card.

To create a large font in Excel, click on the font size and select a number or type in your own. To change the row height and column width, choose 'Format', 'row' and 'height', then 'Format', 'column' and 'width'. The cell shown in Figure 3.4 was formatted using font size 250. The rows were made taller to fit the screen size and the column width set to the width of

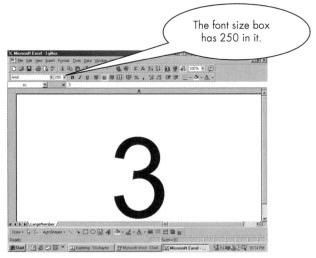

Figure 3.4   Using a spreadsheet to create a large number

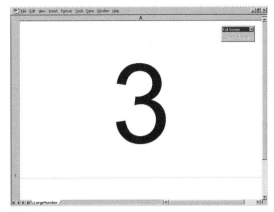

Figure 3.5   The screen after choosing 'view full screen'

the screen. If you choose 'View', 'full screen', some of the distractions disappear (see Figure 3.5). You can type into the cell any number you want to use, depending on the mathematics you want to do. Or you can type in several cells and move between them using the arrow keys. Figure 3.6 shows such an arrangement, viewed at 25 per cent, so that you can see the numbers in the different cells. At 100 per cent you can see only one number at a time.

So what about the mathematics? The National Numeracy Strategy (NNS) (DfEE 1999a) asks for mental skills to be considered in the first part of a lesson: 'The first five to ten minutes of a lesson can be used to rehearse and sharpen skills . . . practising mental calculations and the rapid recall of number facts in varied ways' (p. 13).

There is nothing new in using large numbers, and a flash card showing

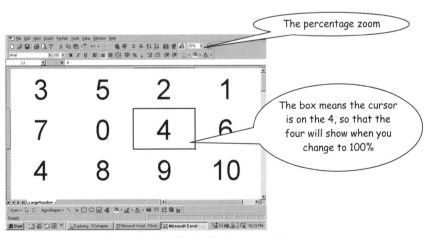

Figure 3.6   Filled cells shown at 25 per cent

a number has long been a favoured tool of teachers. You can show the numbers and get children to chant:

- the number;
- one more than the number;
- two less than the number;
- half the number;
- double the number;
- complements to 10 – the number they would need to add to the number to make 10.

You can, of course, use number cards for quieter activities, such as finding the same number of cubes from a set, or displaying five more than the number on the card on the display of a calculator. If you make cards, however, you have to remember where your put them last time you used them. It can be easier to find your files on a computer.

You could type in the numbers from 1 to 10 for your pupils to read and chant aloud, or to respond with the answer to a times table. Use the cursor keys to move to different cells. Jumble the numbers up so that the pupils will have to think more (as when you shuffle your flash cards).

Fancy fonts

Most packages have fonts that produce symbols or pictures other than those on the keyboard. To change the font, click on the font box and choose from the menu. 'Wingdings' produces some very interesting pictures. You might find them useful when discussing symmetry or time (see Table 3.1).

An alternative is to use a formula, typed into the dialogue box (see Figure 3.7). First, select your cell and choose the Wingdings font from the font menu. Then select the function menu using the 'Fx' button. Then choose the 'text' option. You will be prompted to fill in the character number. Press return and the selected symbol will appear in the cell. Enlarge it to the desired size (see Figure 3.8). Various clock faces are available, showing different times, and coded from 183 to 194.

For short periods of practice, using one computer, you can produce large clock faces on a monitor showing the hour for your younger pupils to chant the time, or two faces to ask how much time has passed.

Table 3.1 Characters using different fonts

Font name									
						Character			
Arial	a	f	J	K	L	Y	Z	–	·
Wingdings	ಹ	↗	☺	☺	☹	✿	☾	✳	☉
Character number in Excel	97	103	74	75	76	89	90	175	183

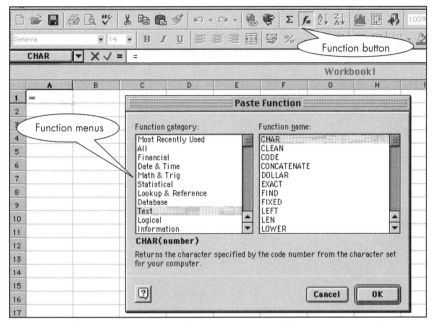

Figure 3.7 Using the function menu to obtain a character

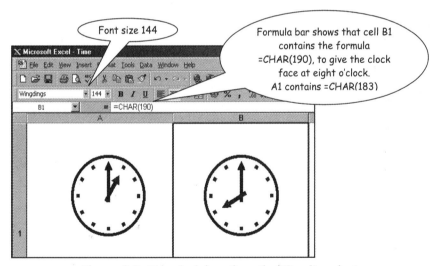

Figure 3.8 Two clock faces from the Wingdings font

Formatting numbers

Excel formats numbers into fractions (be careful that you allow enough figures for the denominators you want to use), decimals (to the number of decimal places you choose) and percentages (to the number of decimal places). This can be useful if you want to practise conversions. To create a fraction, choose 'Format', 'cells', 'number' and 'fraction'. To create a percentage, choose 'Format', 'cells', 'number' and 'percentage'. To change the number of decimal places, choose 'Format', 'cells' and 'general'. 'General' allows different numbers of decimal places whereas 'number' allows you to fix the number of decimal places, which is useful for money (see Figure 3.9).

Each cell can be formatted differently. In Figure 3.10 the cells in column A have the numbers formatted as fractions, column B is general, so that the number of decimal points is not fixed, and in column C the numbers are formatted as percentages with no decimal places. If you type fractions into cells in column A, the equivalent forms appear in columns B and C, thanks to the formula B2 = A2. If you want more rows the cells can be highlighted and copied by dragging down.

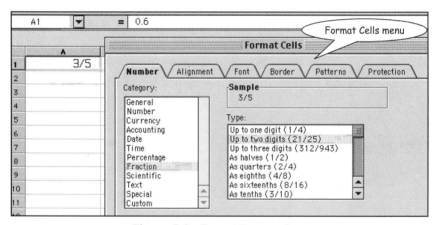

Figure 3.9 Formatting numbers

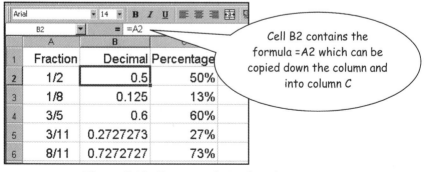

Figure 3.10 Fractions, decimals and percentages

As a short oral activity, ask pupils to suggest fractions that will give 0.7 or 80 per cent, and so on. In the network room, challenge pupils to find as many different fractions which give decimals of the form 0.2, or with a 5 in the hundredths decimal place. Change the formatting if you want to change decimals to fractions or percentages to decimals.

Pictures for numbers

In Excel, charts are called diagrams (see Figures 3.1 and 3.2). How might we use such diagrams, other than for presenting findings from statistical investigations? The most obvious use for a single computer is the pie chart, as its circular representation is very suggestive of the many diagrams we see in textbooks when children are learning about fractions. Figure 3.11 shows how you might set this up. Don't be fooled by the fractions in the diagram – numbers are entered into cells A1 and A2 (in this case 1 and 1) and the number in A3 is the total (in this case 2). A bit of fancy formatting, larger numbers, part of a border to the cell and making row 2 taller gives the appearance of 'fractions'. To get the pie chart, highlight the numbers in A1 and A2 and use the 'chart wizard'. Repeat this with C1 and C2 to get the second pie chart and then with E1 and E2 to get the third. You could have the numbers on a different spreadsheet if you wanted to discuss the diagrams with no number clues!

Templates, such as that shown in Figure 3.11, can be used to demonstrate fractions, to discuss the ratio of the parts of the diagram, the proportions of the sectors, the link to representing data, or pairs of numbers that give diagrams of the same appearance. This last activity is a good one for the network room. Give pupils a template to match diagrams. You can protect a template so that pupils can only type into the cells you want

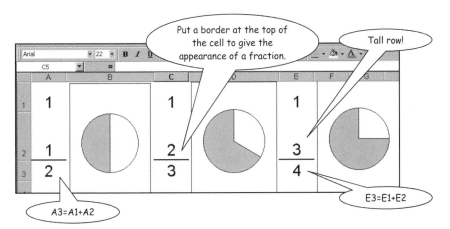

Figure 3.11 Pie charts and fractions

them to. Once a sheet is protected you cannot change the contents of any cell unless you change its formatting. Use the 'Format' menu, and select 'cells' and 'protection' to unlock a cell you want to change. Then protect the sheet by selecting 'Tools' and 'protection'. If you want pages of examples, use a workbook, which is a set of sheets collected together in the same file. Excel opens up workbooks rather than single sheets and extra sheets can be inserted into each workbook.

A Year 5 class used a template like that shown in Figure 3.12 and during the session began to talk about equivalent fractions with enthusiasm, to connect them to their multiplication tables and to use the language of proportion.

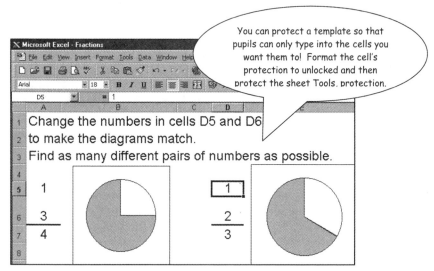

Figure 3.12 A template for exploring equivalent fractions

Generating random numbers

The random number generator in Excel offers the chance to create numbers in a random order. Type '= RAND()' into a cell and press return. A number between 0 and 1 will appear. If you use the F9 key (on a PC) the spreadsheet will recalculate and a different number will appear. Try it. Table 3.2 shows how to create different values of random numbers. If you want whole numbers then use the integer function INT(), with a number inside the brackets. For example INT(17.56) becomes 17. Look at the examples in Table 3.3.

Using the random number generator frees you from repeatedly creating specific sets of numbers. All the activities mentioned in this section can be done using the random number generator.

Table 3.2 Formulae to generate random numbers

=RAND()*5	gives from 0 up to 5, not including 5	e.g. 4.978686
=RAND()*10	gives from 0 up to 10, not including 10	e.g. 8.389087
=RAND()*100	gives from 0 up to 100, not including 100	e.g. 21.456778

Table 3.3 Formulae to generate random integers

=INT(RAND()*10)	0, 1, 2, 3, 4, 5, 6, 7, 8 or 9
=INT(RAND()*100)	0, 1, 2, 3, 4, 5, 6, 7, 8 . . . 98, 99
=INT(RAND()*10) + 1	1, 2, 3, 4, 5, 6, 7, 8, 9 or 10
=10*INT(RAND()*10) + 10	10, 20, 30, 40, 50, 60, 70, 80, 90 or 100
(if you want particular intervals)	

Examples from the NNS

The *Handbook for Leading Mathematics Teachers* (DfEE 1999b: 36) suggests the following as part of a Year 1 lesson:

Add 1 to different numbers that end in 6: 6, 16, 26, 126, 836 . . .
Repeat with other sets of numbers – for example, numbers that end in 0.

Suppose you want the numbers to come from the set 6, 16, 26 . . . 996. That means you want to show one number from a set of 100 numbers, and the formula would look like =10*INT(RAND()*100) + 6. By using a large font, and putting one of the formula into a cell, you can generate a new number from the set every time you press F9, like those in Figure 3.13.

As the numbers are shown on the screen, the pupils can chant the number obtained by adding 1. The task is easily changed to adding or subtracting different numbers – for example, adding 4 might be of interest. Or you may want to use a different set of numbers, in which case all you

Figure 3.13 Creating random numbers ending in 6

have to do is change the formula. For numbers which end in 0 use = 10*INT(RAND()*100).

The *Handbook* (DfEE 1999b: 37) suggests the following activity is used as an introduction to a Year 4 lesson:

> Play 'Number Journeys'. Say: 'Start with 6; subtract 3; add 10; halve the result. What are you left with?' Repeat with other starting numbers and other 'journeys'.

You could use any set of numbers, but as you are using 'halve' you may wish to begin with numbers which will give whole number answers – in this case odd numbers such as 1,3, 5 to 25. The formula for this would be =2*INT(RAND()*13) + 1. If you wanted the half to appear in the response every time then you could always begin with even numbers by using: =2*INT(RAND()*15) + 2.

Your choice of the set of numbers to use focuses on the mathematical attributes of the task. A journey such as 'add 3, divide by 7, subtract 1' would offer whole number answers for 4, 11,18 and 25, so you could use =7*INT(RAND()*15) + 4.

The advantage of using a spreadsheet for this activity, rather than flash cards, is that you are more likely to focus on a particular set of numbers for the mathematical purpose of the task, because the formula expects you to make those mathematical decisions. The formula can be generalized as: *difference**INT(RAND()**number of numbers*) + *starting number*.

The type of numbers you choose to use can help you to recognize the mathematical implications of the activity. If you are working on carrying, you may always want your numbers to end in 7 for adding on 5, 6, 7 etc. In this case you would use the formula =10*INT(RAND()*15) + 7. By thinking about the number set you wish to use you are focusing on the nature of 'carry' and counting on from 7.

One teacher was working on 'double, double', initially using whole numbers to stress the relationship with multiples of four. She later used 0.25*INT(RAND()*20) + 0.25. Initially, pupils used calculators to work on the doubling and doubling, eventually realizing that they always got whole numbers. The question then was why. Why do numbers such as 3.75 give a whole number when you double and double? What does 0.25 have to do with a quarter?

You may want to create large numbers for reading aloud – say the numbers between 20 and 50 inclusive (31 numbers), or numbers ending in 0.5, or numbers ending in 000. Table 3.4 provides the relevant formulae.

Table 3.4 Ranges of random numbers

20 to 50	=INT(RAND()*31) + 20
40 numbers from 0.5	=INT(RAND()*40) + 0.5
Numbers ending in 000	=1000*INT(RAND()*20)+1000

Table 3.5 Combining ranges of random numbers

Set of numbers wanted	107, 102, 405, 307	1003, 2067, 9034
Split into two or more sets	100, 200, 300 . . . plus 0, 1 . . . 9	1000, 2000, 3000 . . . plus 0, 1 . . . 99
Formulae to create the sets	=100*INT(RAND()*8+1) + INT(RAND()*10)	=1000*INT(RAND()*8+1) + INT(RAND()*100)

A good activity for chanting is reading sets of numbers such as 107, 102, 405, 307 or 1003, 2067, 9034. You can create such numbers for practising reading these types of numbers by combining formulae, such as those shown in Table 3.5.

What about using numbers to tell the time? For digital clocks your random numbers would need two cells, one for the hours (12 or 24?) and one for the minutes. (A third cell can be used for the colon symbol ':' to make the whole thing look more real.) Use a large font. A little more formatting is necessary if you want the usual two-figure appearance – for example, 02. You can format numbers like those shown in Figure 3.14 by using the 'Format' menu: 'cells', 'number', 'custom'. Then type '00'.

Sequences

There are times when you will need a specific sequence of numbers and not a random selection. For a sample Year 2 lesson, the *Handbook* (DfEE 1999b: 36) gives the introduction as:

> In unison, count from 0 in ones, twos and fives as high as the class can go, and back to 0.

Before children are ready to do this activity without any cues, it can be useful to chant along with the number on the screen. Enter the formula

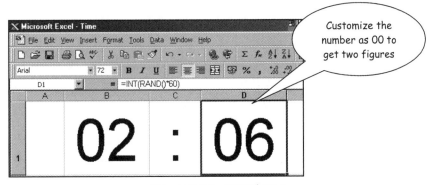

Figure 3.14 Digital time

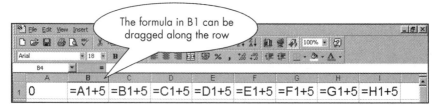

Figure 3.15   Formulae for an 'add 5' sequence

(=A1+5) in B1, copy/drag the formula across the row and then make the font large enough to show only one cell at a time (see Figure 3.15). By moving along the cells, you can control the speed of the chanting. Stop at different numbers and ask for predictions of the next numbers. Move backwards and forwards to look at patterns such as 5, 10, 15, 20, 25, 20, 15, 10, and so on. If you type a different number into A1, you will have a whole new sequence to explore. Other 'add 5' patterns might be 2, 7, 12 or 3, 8, 13, 18. Children can follow the sequence using a calculator, by typing in the starting number, followed by '+ +', followed by the added number (in this case, 5). Pressing '=' will then add the number automatically.

A suggested start for a Year 4 lesson (DfEE, 1999b: 37) is:

Chant the four times-table, forwards and backwards.

and the introduction to a Year 5 lesson (DfEE 1999b: 38) is similar:

Chant the six times-table, forwards and backwards.

You can easily change the formula to 'add 4' or 'add 6'. Alternatively, you can devise templates to add any sequence, using what is known as 'absolute' and 'relative' referencing. In Figure 3.16, the use of the $ sign means that when the formula is dragged the 'B1' does not change (absolute referencing) but the 'A2' does – to B2, C2 and so on (relative referencing). The formula in Figure 3.16 currently gives an 'add 6' sequence (see

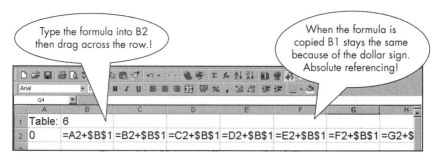

Figure 3.16   Using a cell to store the difference

	A	B	C	D	E	F	G	H
1	Table:	6						
2	0	6	12	18	24	30	36	42

Figure 3.17 An 'add 6' sequence

Figure 3.17), but this is easily changed. The difference between terms is stored in B1. If B1 is changed to 4, then an 'add 4' sequence will result. You can format the size of the cells to show one, two or three numbers at a time according to how you want to work on the sequence.

The *Handbook* (DfEE 1999b: 38) suggests the following to start a Year 6 lesson:

> Start off some number sequences for the class to continue, for example:
> 7, 10, 13, 16 . . .
> 235, 245, 255, 265 . . .
> 91, 88, 85, 82 . . .

There are many occasions when you may want to practise sequences, and sequences are what spreadsheets seem to be designed for. It is easy to set up a formula and drag it along rows or down columns. Such sequences can be used as a starter, with pupils chanting the next term, predicting the term after or reading the sequences to practise tables. Alternatively, if your pupils are working individually or in pairs at a machine, you could ask them to devise their own sequences. Challenges might include:

- Find ten sequences with 7 as the fifth number, record the tenth number each time. Now can you create that sequence?
- Find ten sequences with 8.5 as the third number.
- Find some sequences with 17 in them: one where it is the third term, one where it is the fourth, one the fifth and so on. What connections are there between your sequences? In what different ways can this be done?

Number grids

Sequences can be extended into two dimensions, creating the ever-popular number grids, for which there are many examples in the NNS. You can easily create them on a spreadsheet and print off copies for the pupils to use. They are really only sequences collected together. The *Handbook* (DfEE 1999b: 41) suggests the following exercises using a 100 grid, the formulae for which are shown in Figure 3.18:

> Lesson 3 Use the 100 grid to demonstrate adding 9 to two-digit numbers, progressing to subtracting 9.

> Once you have a formula drag across to fill a row, drag down to fill columns

Arial			10		B	I	U	≣ ≣ ≣	⊞	🕮 %

	K10	▼	=						

	A	B	C	D	E	F	G	H	I	J
1	1	=A1+1	=B1+1	=C1+1	=D1+1	=E1+1	=F1+1	=G1+1	=H1+1	=I1+1
2	=A1+10	=B1+10	=C1+10	=D1+10	=E1+10	=F1+10	=G1+10	=H1+10	=I1+10	=J1+10
3	=A2+10	=B2+10	=C2+10	=D2+10	=E2+10	=F2+10	=G2+10	=H2+10	=I2+10	=J2+10
4	=A3+10	=B3+10	=C3+10	=D3+10	=E3+10	=F3+10	=G3+10	=H3+10	=I3+10	=J3+10
5	=A4+10	=B4+10	=C4+10	=D4+10	=E4+10	=F4+10	=G4+10	=H4+10	=I4+10	=J4+10
6	=A5+10	=B5+10	=C5+10	=D5+10	=E5+10	=F5+10	=G5+10	=H5+10	=I5+10	=J5+10
7	=A6+10	=B6+10	=C6+10	=D6+10	=E6+10	=F6+10	=G6+10	=H6+10	=I6+10	=J6+10
8	=A7+10	=B7+10	=C7+10	=D7+10	=E7+10	=F7+10	=G7+10	=H7+10	=I7+10	=J7+10
9	=A8+10	=B8+10	=C8+10	=D8+10	=E8+10	=F8+10	=G8+10	=H8+10	=I8+10	=J8+10
10	=A9+10	=B9+10	=C9+10	=D9+10	=E9+10	=F9+10	=G9+10	=H9+10	=I9+10	=J9+10

Figure 3.18 Formulae for a 100 grid

Lesson 4 Use the 100 grid to demonstrate addition and subtraction of multiples of 10 to and from any two-digit number, for example, 23 + 20, 72 − 30, and so on.

If you need more numbers, it is easy to drag down the formulae to make the grid go up to 1000 or more.

Pat was working with a Year 4 class, using calculators to investigate the pattern created when you add 1 to numbers ending in 9. The pupils had written:

9 + 1 = 10
19 + 1 = 20
29 + 1 = 30
39 + 1 = 40, and so on.

They had looked at the pattern on the hundred grid and were using the language of units digits, tens digits etc. The problem came after '99 + 1 = 100' when, instead of the expected '109 + 1' many pupils wrote '1009 + 1 = ?'.

This is a common misunderstanding among pupils, but extending beyond the 100 grid will help (why do we always stop at 100?). The next day Pat took in a number grid that was ten columns wide but went up to 310 (it used a small font, and was created using a spreadsheet). The children became really excited by the patterns in the numbers beyond 100. Their language was extended to larger numbers and they were delighted that they could begin to predict for larger numbers.

In the Year 6 lesson (DfEE 1999b: 38) a main activity given is:

Pupils draw a 5 × 5 grid on squared paper and in the bottom left hand square they write 1. They are to make up a rule for going up and another one for going to the right. The aim is to fill up the grid using these two rules. Stop the class and ask for two volunteers to describe patterns and relationships in all eight directions on their grids. Now challenge the pupils to produce individually a new grid with more complex rules such as using larger numbers, multiplying, starting in the middle square . . .

You could use a computer in the classroom to set up this activity with a pre-prepared grid. Figure 3.19 shows the grid proposed by the NNS and the beginnings of the same grid using a spreadsheet. We would probably start from the top left, so we could drag the sequences or use formulae. Pupils could then work in pairs or groups and the ideas could be discussed and illustrated using the computer. The mathematics remains as was intended in the original task, and the computer offers a quick method for pupils to produce their own grids to tests hypotheses before sharing them with the class. The computer and a large screen allow much easier public sharing and discussion of ideas.

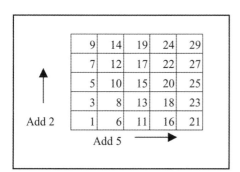
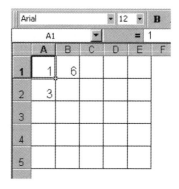

Figure 3.19 Creating a number grid on a spreadsheet

This could also be an activity for the network room, where pupils could produce their grids by dragging or using formulae. The focus is then much more on the formation of formulae – the short representation of the mathematics of the task – which replaces the sentences used to describe the pencil and paper version.

Filling in operation tables can be a useful short activity for the beginning of a lesson (or at any time when you want a change of pace). Figures 3.20 and 3.21 show how to set up an operation table spreadsheet, for instant display on the screen for whole-class discussion or as lots of printed versions. Try connecting two sheets so that you have the answers on a separate sheet using linked formulae. Figure 3.21 shows how the formulae connect sheets 3 and 4 in Figure 3.20. Sheet 3 is for the students to see and sheet 4 has the answers so you could show this sheet if you wanted pupils to mark their own work. If you change sheet 3 the next day, the answer sheet will also change, saving a lot of work. You might want to use random numbers in the table headings or type them in yourself. Figure

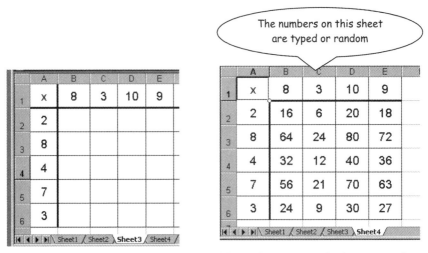

Figure 3.20 Making an operations table (in this case a multiplication grid)

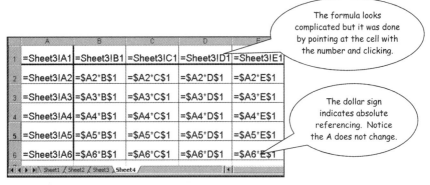

Figure 3.21 Formulae for the multiplication grid

3.21 also shows some more absolute referencing: '=$A2*B$1' means that when the formula is copied to other cells the A and the 1 will remain unchanged but the 2 and the B will change to suit the new cell position.

Developing visual imagery

The spreadsheet can also be used to develop 'pictures' of numbers. The one we are most used to is the dice (see Figure 3.22) and we owe this image to Neville and Tyrrell (see Tyrrell 1996).

To create the face of a dice in Excel, you can use the Wingdings font to represent the dots, using CHAR(108). Table 3.6 shows how to fill in the

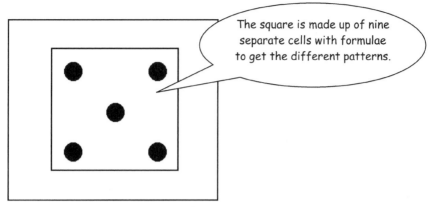

Figure 3.22 The face of a dice, created in Excel

cells. In cell B1, type in the formula to create a random number from 1 to 6. The dice face is formed in the nine cells A2: C4. The formula in cell A2 checks B1 to see if the value is greater than 3. If so, then a dot goes into cell A2. If not, the cell is left blank.

You can use the computer-generated dice for chanting exercises. Recognizing the number of dots is very different from recognizing the numeral.

Other images can be valuable in developing number sense – for example, those on playing cards, the abacus or the ten frame: 'Considerable emphasis is being given in American arithmetic instruction to developing number concepts by associating quantities with visual images. For example, single and double ten frames are becoming increasingly common in American textbooks' (Yackel 2000: 27). You can create a ten frame using formulae like those shown in Figure 3.23. Set up a cell with a random number formula (1–10) on a part of the spreadsheet you cannot see. Name the cell 'num 1' by using the 'Insert' menu and selecting 'name' and 'define'. The formulae required to put dots in the right cells, if the conditional statement is true, can also be seen in Figure 3.23.

Possible uses of the ten frame include counting in twos, the recognition

Table 3.6 Formulae to create a dice face

	A	B	C
1		=INT(RAND()*6) + 1	
2	=IF(B1>3,CHAR(108), "")		=IF(B1>1,CHAR(108), "")
3	=IF(B1=6,CHAR(108), "")	=IF(OR((B1=1), (B1=3),(B1=5)), CHAR(108), "")	=IF(B1=6,CHAR(108), "")
4	=IF(B1>1,CHAR(108), "")		=IF(B1>3,CHAR(108), "")

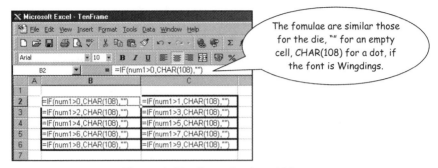

The fomulae are similar those for the die, "" for an empty cell, CHAR(108) for a dot, if the font is Wingdings.

Figure 3.23   Formulae for a 10 frame

of odd and even numbers and strategies for visualizing numbers. Complements to 10 are an obvious activity once children begin to recognize the pattern of dots. The images – easily changed using F9 – can be used for practice, discussion about number or perhaps about probability – higher or lower! With two frames you can compare the numbers, working on difference, or discuss their sum. You might ask questions about fractions, ratio and scale as well as the number operations. This type of template is probably more useful for oral work or plenaries than work in the network room (see Figure 3.24).

Finally, for pupils in Key Stage 2, graphs of sequences can extend mathematical imagery. One of the most useful images in mathematics is that of the coordinate diagram and an arithmetic sequence can be illustrated as sets of coordinate pairs (position in sequence/term) using a scatter diagram (see Figure 3.25). These images for sequences are very powerful, as well as being an important link to equations of lines and

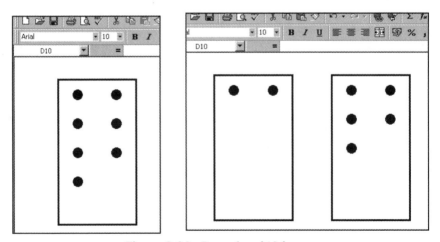

Figure 3.24   Examples of 10 frames

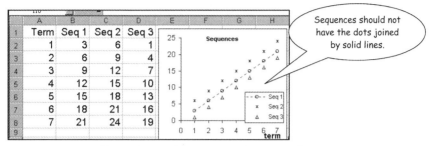

Figure 3.25   Sequences and a scatter diagram

curves. For some children this image might help their understanding of equal steps. You can join the points with a dotted line to help the visual impact of the sequence.

Using data

It is well known that Excel can produce lots of diagrams, but the challenge for teaching is to help pupils to select an *appropriate* diagram – one that illustrates the mathematics they are learning. Working on such choice can provide lots of opportunities for discussion. The following example could be an excellent starter: 'When, and why would you choose pie charts or a column graph for the data from 'The World Guide?' (see Figure 3.26). Data like this, which is suitable for discussion, can be found on the web,

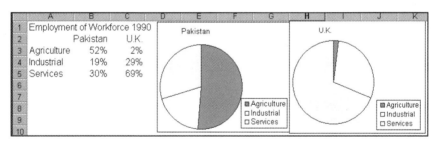

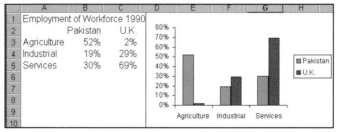

Figure 3.26   Using a pie chart and a column graph to represent the same data

but children could also collect their own. For example, working in small groups, using no rulers or other measuring equipment, each pupil cuts some pieces of string to measurements of 3cm, 5cm 8cm, 10cm and 15cm. They then stick the string onto paper so that it is straight, and label it the size they think it is. Each member of the group measures everyone's string and comes to an agreement about the actual length, and then fills in a table with their estimates. The data can then be entered onto a spreadsheet and diagrams produced for different individuals for the class to compare. Are the class underestimators or overestimators on average? How else might the data be represented? Get the children to practise measuring, then do the task again. Has practice made them better estimators? This task offers each person enough purposeful work to do and the data can be entered onto the spreadsheet as they are working, making a single computer a useful resource.

Pratt (1995) offers examples of ideas used in primary classrooms, such as body measurements or the flight of paper spinners. He also highlights the difference between passive graphing, when the only purpose is to produce a diagram and active graphing, when the diagram is used to explore and analyse the data rather than simply represent it. The purpose of the diagrams in the string task is to compare performances, and it is the discussion of the comparisons and the evidence for them that offers a mathematical approach.

Spreadsheets do challenge the need to produce diagrams by hand, but they also reinforce the need to know what the diagrams *mean* and how to interpret them.

Lots of practice

The one thing a spreadsheet program will never tire of is producing numbers, and there are lots of opportunities for number practice in the network room. The children (as when they are using calculators) should not be producing answers, but working on challenges which develop number sense and encourage their estimation and number-pattern skills. You could ask them to find fractions which add up to a half, or decimals which add up to numbers with an 8 in the the hundredths place (see Figure 3.27), either by producing a template or by teaching the pupils to produce their own.

	A	B	C	D	E	F
E1		=	=A1+C1			
1	1/4	+	1/4	=	1/2	
2	3/8	+	1/8	=	1/2	
3	1/12	+	5/12	=	1/2	
4		+		=		

	A	B	C	D	E
E1		=	=A1+C1		
1	0.34	+	0.24	=	0.58
2	0.356	+	0.231	=	0.587
3	0.903	+	0.184	=	1.087
4		+		=	0

Figure 3.27   Exploring decimals and fractions

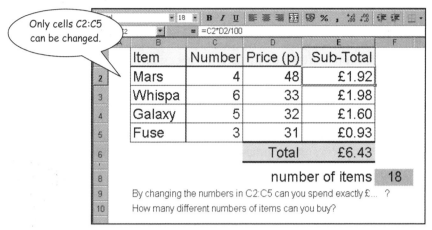

Figure 3.28 Shopping template

Many calculator activities can be used with spreadsheets, the advantage being that the children can have a printed record of their work. The advantage over written recording is that wrong ideas can be quickly over-written. The example in Figure 3.28 uses a large font, which we find useful in the network room because you can easily read pupils' work from a distance, making monitoring easier.

You may not have access to a computer room, but you may nevertheless want to produce some practice sheets. Using some random numbers and a bit of formatting, you can produce lots of different sheets like those in Figure 3.27, or more traditional question and answer sheets. Remember to produce answer sheets for yourself (see Figures 3.20 and 3.21).

You may want to try a different type of problem, and such sheets can be designed to produce arrays or tables for pupils to explore. You might set up a magic square or consider the shopping task in Figure 3.28. This was one of the first problems we used in primary schools: the task was to spend exactly £7. It was fascinating to watch those who could solve the problem quickly, moving in and out of context, sometimes asking for another Mars bar, sometimes for 50p. Others were firmly in context, only talking about 'Give me another Fuse' or even saying that they would not spend that much on chocolate (Perks and Prestage 1994)! Those pupils who are good mathematically are pupils who use the context when it is useful, but ignore it and stick to the numbers when they realize that this is the easiest way to complete the task.

You may be able to adapt many of the problems in your textbooks to suit this type of exploratory mathematics. The book *From Little Acorns* (Ravenscroft *et al.* 1996) offers some useful problems and provides help in setting up the required spreadsheets.

Spreadsheets with everything?

This chapter has suggested some ideas of how you might use spreadsheets in lessons – for starters, for plenaries, for exploring and practising, and so on. Much of what we do does not change the mathematics, but the spreadsheet does add other dimensions such as speed, the ability to vary numbers quickly, to explore lots of data, record and represent. Spreadsheets offer a useful resource to produce data and discuss it with pupils, to make printed sheets, to set tasks for pupils to explore and to provide the opportunity to practise lots of the mathematics curriculum.

References

DfEE (Department for Education and Employment) (1999a) *The National Numeracy Strategy: Framework for Teaching Mathematics from Reception to Year 6*. Cambridge: Cambridge University Press.

DfEE (Department for Education and Employment) (1999b) *Handbook for Leading Mathematics Teachers*. Barnet: DfEE/BEAM Education.

Perks, P. and Prestage, S. (1994) Shopping with spreadsheets, *Micromath*, 10(3): 33–6.

Pratt, D. (1995) Young children's active and passive graphing, *Journal of Computer Assisted Learning*, 11(3): 157–69.

Ravenscroft, L., Cobden, D., Abell, C. and Griffin, E. (1996) *From Little Acorns: Spreadsheets 9 to 13*. Leicester: The Mathematical Association.

Tyrrell, S. (1996) Statistics using spreadsheets, *Micromath*, 12(2): 32–6.

Yackel, E. (2000) Perspectives on arithmetic from classroom-based research in the USA, in J. Anghileri (ed.) *Principles and Practices in Arithmetic Teaching: Innovative Practices for the Primary Classroom*. Buckingham: Open University Press.

4

LEARNING TECHNOLOGIES, LEARNING STYLES AND LEARNING MATHEMATICS

John Vincent

Introduction

National Curriculum, numeracy blocks, time constraints, large classes? How can we fit computers into mathematics in the primary school? Is there room? Is there time? Is there a need? Such questions are constantly being asked in these and similar forms.

This chapter suggests some of the reasons why the computer needs to become an essential integrated part of the mathematics curriculum – but not just the computer. The right software and an appropriate open-learning environment are perhaps even more important, a point that is discussed at the end of the chapter. This chapter mainly looks at how children can respond to one particular piece of open, constructivist software, MicroWorlds.

Of the reasons in favour of computers touched on here, one that is highly important is learning styles. All children learn in different ways, but in a big, crowded classroom we need all the help we can get to operate a learning environment that provides access to mathematics for all children, whatever their learning style. Those that need this help most are those with a strongly preferred visual style, a group we fail miserably in many classrooms. The computer as a source of help for all learning styles is examined. In addition there is the matter of the computer as an extension of our intelligence, the issue of enthusing talented children and the role of the computer and challenging software in achieving this. The chapter also raises the idea of computers as partners in learning, including the computer as a neutral friend for those who are afraid to be wrong.

Learning styles

Primary mathematics is a hybrid endeavour. It demands substantial use of verbal faculties, the logical symbolism of numbers, spatial symbolism and visual skills. There are two particular problems with this analysis.

One problem is the nature of teaching. Teachers tend to be verbal people, to rely heavily on words and verbal delivery styles. It is possibly why they become teachers – they want to 'teach' in the sense that they want to impart knowledge. To support the verbal nature of teaching mathematics, mathematics teaching is full of words. Mathematics textbooks are word-heavy, mathematics problems are verbally mediated and classroom mathematics tends to be explained and introduced with words.

However, many children do not naturally learn verbally. There is a good deal of evidence from cognitive psychology, from neuropsychology and from observations in the classroom by serving teachers that in any one classroom there is a multitude of different preferred ways of learning. These learning styles appear largely to be responses by learners to natural individual differences in cognitive styles. It is not the purpose of this chapter to examine the possible reasons for this. The neuropsychology arguments can be followed in publications such as Ornstein (1997) and Gazzaniga (1998). Work on the analysis and assessment of cognitive styles has been summarized clearly by Riding and Raynor (1998), and the interested reader is pointed in that direction. Here it is assumed that variations in cognitive style exist, probably on two continuums – from verbal to visual on one, and from holistic to analytic on the other.

There is a real danger that in the normal classroom there will be a mismatch between the learning styles of a number of the children and the learning scaffolded by the teacher, unless the teacher is aware of these styles and the right learning environment has been established to cater for all the children. Some children, who are at the visual end of a verbal-visual cognitive style spectrum (Riding and Raynor 1998) probably do not have the learning style strategies to cope with the verbal delivery of mathematics. Such children were being highlighted in the 1980s by writers such as Dixon (1983) and Sinatra (1986) who referred to them as 'visual children'. Because of the state of understanding of cognitive styles at the time, this was probably somewhat simplistic. Nevertheless such writers recognized that in our classrooms there are some children who need visual means of both constructing learning and of expressing themselves.

There are other children that Riding and Raynor (1998) would categorize on the holistic-analytic spectrum, as being at the analytic end. If they are both at the analytic end and the verbal end of the respective cognitive styles, dealing with visual and holistic elements in mathematics is likely to be stressful. Such children may work comfortably with analytical and logical problems, but become frustrated, for example, when presented with a problem involving visualization of shapes in a three-dimensional pattern.

The ease of mathematical assimilation by primary children depends upon the learning style of the child, in a magic fusion with the teaching style of the teacher. Whether the magic is white or black depends on this interlacing of learning and teaching styles. Because of the heavy imbalance of verbal learning styles and didactic teaching styles among teachers, children at the visual end of the spectrum may suffer from a lack of understanding of their needs. There is a danger in education, arising from the verbal dominance of its practitioners, of establishing a hierarchy of learning styles where we see one style, usually the verbal one, as being superior or more effective.

A number of writers have taken up the theme of the dearth of visual learning techniques in mathematics. Goldenberg (1995) wrote of the remarkable effects of dynamic geometry software on some secondary children who strongly preferred to think and work in a visual way and more recently has highlighted the way that mathematics teaching can miss whole sections of the student body if it does not address the visual issues:

> Some students who would like a visually rich mathematics never find out that there is one because they've already dropped out before they've had the chance to encounter any of the visual elements. We lose not only potential geometers and topologists in this way, but all students who might enter mathematics through its visually richer domains and then discover other worlds, not as intrinsically visual, to which they can apply their visual abilities and inclinations.
>
> (Goldenberg *et al.* 1998: 5)

Computers as extensions of intelligence

The early writers on visually preferred learning styles were writing before the impact of the newest technologies, some of which are beginning to make a significant impact on the provision of learning environments. For the first time in the history of mass education we have the tool that can give the teacher the means of providing a learning environment for all learning styles. It is called the computer. Many have now recognized that computers are already having a major influence on the way we learn and consequently what we learn. Mathematicians in particular have commented on the revolution at whose centre we stand. Kaput (2000), for example, is one of a number of writers who have proposed that the human race is on the cusp of a huge change. He isolates a number of seminal changes to technology in the history of mankind that have each marked an extension in the intellectual ability of the human mind. To Kaput it is not what you do with the tools, it is how the technology has extended our human minds. He writes of the invention of a phonetic writing script; the invention of a place value number system with a zero place holder; the spread of mass printing; and the invention of algebra as the major points of change. The next major change is the one we are witnessing: the introduction of cheap, dynamic computational media. The older technologies were 'instantiated in and hence subject to the constraints of the static, inert media of the previous several millennia. But the computational medium is neither static nor inert, but rather is dynamic and interactive' (Kaput 2000: 7).

Computers as partners in learning

There is a growing body of educators who are seeing computers as a natural part of the learning environment in which the learner is part of a network of learning. The computer is also part of this network – a partner in learning. Goody (1977) calls the major jumps in learning tools 'technologies of the intellect'. Today it is the computer which is the core of these new technologies. With that tool has come software that can either negate all the potential that the computer has to liberate children, or activate it. But it must be used in a very open-ended and creative way, where play and freedom to experiment without penalty are coexistent conditions. To allow students to experiment and problem-set, they must have software that is compatible with those aims. Some would call these constructivist conditions. Most of the stories that follow have arisen from the use of a piece of software, called MicroWorlds, which is not very commonly used in British primary schools, although it has been enthusiastically adopted in some parts of North America, Japan and Australia. It is multimedia software with a simple programming base of the Logo language and is a real catalyst for change and growth. However, MicroWorlds is not so unique that other applications cannot be used in some of the ways discussed here. A great deal can be done with modern word processors and with spreadsheets. Any multimedia environment has some of the potentials of MicroWorlds to address the learning needs of all children. There are simple ones such as Textease and Kidpix, commercial display applications such as Microsoft PowerPoint and some of the attractive and more recent versions of Logo that take the pain out of programming while providing a visual richness. For a very easy (and free!)

adaptation of Logo, download Spike Logo from the NRICH mathematics site (www.nrich.maths.org.uk).

MicroWorlds is a full multimedia application and hence has far more uses than just in mathematics. It is frequently used for language and project display work, where its visual features and animation possibilities captivate children. For mathematics, its visual richness is also important and a real bonus is that Logo is used as its scripting language, for Logo is inherently mathematical. Since the application is entirely open-ended (it does not even come with a manual, although children soon find the help screens) it is made to be used in an open, exploratory way. The stories told here are of children who have been taught very little about MicroWorlds, but have taught themselves (and their teachers). They have started with simple problems and then set themselves more and more complex ones.

The case of the visual child

Nathan was a young man of few words. He was a 10-year-old student who rarely spoke in class, avoided all writing if he could and found any Mathematics involving language or rote learning very hard. He had a severe spelling deficit, and did not know his tables or other number bonds. Vincent (2000) reported that Nathan was a student in a class in which all children had frequent access to laptop computers, and, crucially, access to software for mathematics that was visually and mathematically rich. In primary classes few programs fit this description, but MicroWorlds certainly does. Nathan had had exposure to MicroWorlds. The teacher had allowed all the children to play with its possibilities. Very little 'teaching' of the Logo language behind the program had taken place, but Nathan, together with many others, had been experimenting with the animation and visual features non-stop in his spare time. His teacher had set a challenge to make a slide show of polygons, following work on a 'total turtle trip' (to draw any polygon with Logo the turtle must make a total turning trip of 360 degrees). The teacher was working with another child when he heard a melody on a computer in the rhythm of a samba. He moved to investigate, to find that Nathan had produced a 'film' of six polygons appearing on the screen and dancing to the rhythm of the samba tune that he had found in the resources folder of the program. The extensive programming that went into his 'dancing polygons' involved language, logical sequencing and step-by step reasoning – all activities for which he had shown neither inclination nor ability (see Figure 4.1).

Nathan could be characterized as having a visually preferred learning style. He certainly found any language work hard going, yet this program provided a launching pad for logic, language (through a computer programming language) and step-by-step reasoning. Why was this? Could it be a visual medium for learning interceding on behalf of logic and

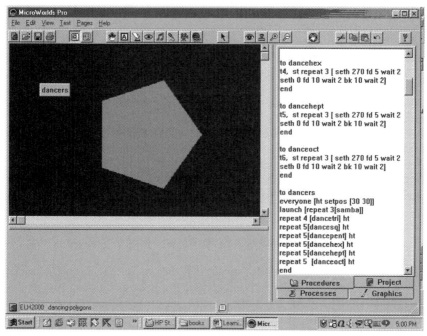

Figure 4.1   Sample page and part of the procedure for Nathan's 'dancing polygons'

sequential reasoning? Much work suggesting that this indeed can be the case has been done by neuropsychologists with language, and there is no doubt that it applies equally well to mathematics. Ornstein (1997: 176), for example, following his own work with humour and that of others with metaphor, came to the conclusion that the right hemisphere of the brain is not only the seat of visual processing, but acts as the 'stage' upon which full meaning is constructed. Chiarello (1998), another neuropsychologist working with language, suggests that the right and left hemispheres of the brain access information in quite different ways, with the right hemisphere being vital to establishing whole meaning. Some children apparently need a strongly visual (right brain) input to mediate their learning through the left brain.

An Australian sports fan

The class was asked to demonstrate the nature of fractions using Micro-Worlds. Kathy had a dislike for language work, a severe spelling deficit and a difficulty expressing herself in mathematics. She had low self-esteem because much in school that gave her feedback on her worth depended on either expression of language or of written mathematics. She had a short attention span and a poor distraction index. She did have a talent for art and like many Australian students, male or female, was a fanatical supporter of a football team. During the class work on fractions with MicroWorlds, she worked long and hard without a single distraction except when others, who now saw Kathy as an 'expert', asked her for advice. Her fractions outcome was in the form of a teaching unit for children who did not understand and it alternated a 'learning' page with a 'play' page. Figure 4.2 does not do the work justice, as no screen dump from MicroWorlds can indicate the animations, the sounds and the programming details, but it is plain that a great deal of visual planning has been used. More than that, however, is the understanding that has been demonstrated, and the fact that the original problem has been taken, shaken and greatly deepened. It included equivalence, a concept that had not been met at this stage. Kathy had gone to a book to discover this, checking it with the teacher as she progressed.

Harel and Papert (1991: 48) reported on a similar development in a primary class when Harel studied the use of Logo for working with fractions. They commented on how one girl, Debbie, was quite impervious to the mathematics work on fractions until she realized the possibilities of using Logo. Like Kathy she devised a set of teaching screens for others to use and found that fractions came alive. While Harel and Papert do not talk of children with strongly visual learning styles, reading their report one gets the strong impression of a child with a strongly preferred visual learning style, disinterested in traditional classroom 'left-brain oriented' learning situations. Debbie was then allowed to explore, using the visual construction elements of Logo, and straight away saw fractions in a holistic, integrated way, not analytically. Harel's thesis was that the constructionist environment mediated Debbie's outcomes. An additional interpretation could be that the computer and Logo seemed to mediate an understanding of fractions through visual stimulus – Ornstein's 'stage' again.

The case of the verbal child

Amanda was a skilled language practitioner. She was in the same Grade 5 class as Nathan but there the similarities ended. She could bend the English language to her will. The teacher was first alerted to Amanda's problem with visual learning when she was asked to illustrate while she wrote. She prevaricated and tried to avoid the task. In mathematics her number work was efficient and her number facts and algorithm understanding were excellent, and she devoted her mathematics life to 'getting it right'. Because of this, problem-solving of any sort was never really attempted unless she could see the solution very quickly. If she couldn't

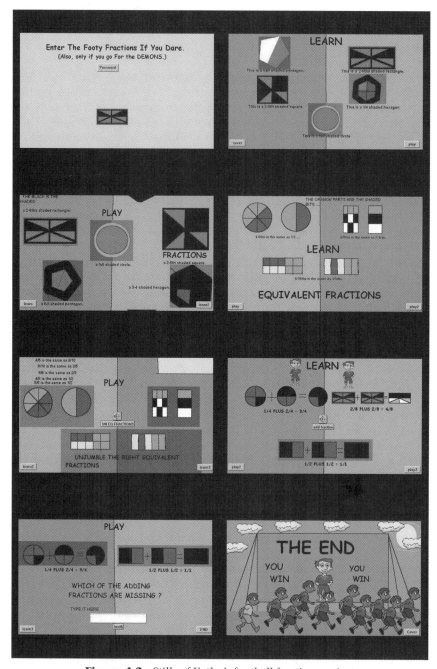

Figure 4.2 Stills of Kathy's football fraction project

get it right in a few minutes she became frustrated and gave up. In spatial work she was at sea. The visually rich MicroWorlds program and constant access to the computer performed a quite different role for Amanda than for Nathan.

Anna Sfard (Sfard and Leron 1996), studying students working at mathematics problems without the computer and with it, comes to the conclusion that the computer provides a different culture in miniature. She suggests that the traditional mathematics classroom is an environment where it is not easy to be wrong, where pressure to be right induces tension and easy give-up on problems. Computers on the other hand offer chances for steps with errors that can be corrected on the way to refining a solution: 'Traversing the short distance between the math classroom and the computer lab was, in fact, a journey between two different worlds, governed by completely different norms and beliefs' (Sfard and Leron 1996: 191). Sfard believes that the computer brings a promise of fair play where, like in real life, difficult problems are not solved in one shot.

Amanda came to see the computer as a neutral friend where ideas could be tried and if they didn't work it was between her and the computer. So she would try again. The simple Logo programming techniques of MicroWorlds allowed her to build her solutions to problems upon

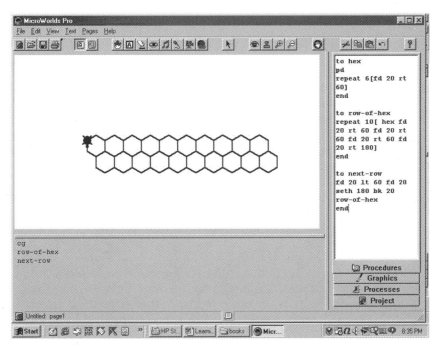

Figure 4.3 Amanda's procedure for a honeycomb pattern

the mistakes she had made in the programming. Each mistake was a step in the process. However, the teacher had to keep out of this process – as soon as he tried to intervene, the shutters went up. Intervention equalled interference. One day, Amanda was working on a tessellation problem using Logo to draw a series of tessellating hexagons like a honeycomb. The teacher very surreptitiously passed by her desk several times, curious as to how she was coping. At the end of the first row there is a programming problem of how to turn the turtle round to nest the second row on top. Amanda tried several times with trial and error, quite happy to make mistakes. Suddenly one trial gave the clue she wanted, and she triumphantly programmed in the correct turn (see Figure 4.3). She had used the visual and programming facilities to mediate a problem that her verbal learning style could not cope with.

Amanda went on to set her own problems with MicroWorlds and then solve them. Although most of her work was language based (she came to love creating animated children's stories), the programming involved was inherently mathematical. One stunning production was a rewrite of the Sleeping Beauty folk tale called 'Drowsy Dreadful' in which the programming of bearings, coordinates, angles, polygons and other spatial concepts was incorporated. Of course, Amanda would never admit that this was mathematics!

The case of the talented ones

The release that the computer and the MicroWorlds environment gave to Amanda was by removing the shackles of being wrong. For Rob and Cath it was the ability to escape from the mediocre by setting their own problems and then solving them. What the computer does with open-ended software is to let very talented students experiment and test their abilities against a 'neutral' opponent whom they recognize as a challenger that is totally fair. If they make a mistake they have only them-selves to blame. The computer is scrupulously honest about it, but does not criticize. In 1990, Steve Costa was involved in the planning for a scheme for a class of 10-year-olds at a Melbourne private school to have their own laptop computers. In 2000 he reflected on one of the changes that the computer made:

> Often by taking a risk and 'getting it wrong' the student's learning became more real and personal. Mistakes were now seen as having beneficial side effects. They often led to further efforts and research, and, as a consequence, a lesson was being learned firsthand that errors can help us to see the 'right way'.
>
> (Costa 2000: 70)

Very talented children can afford to play creatively on the computer without fear of it complaining, and then they can set problems that will challenge their own abilities.

Rob was a student with multiple abilities but a very special affinity for visual presentations. He had some language weaknesses of which he was deeply sensitive and defensive. He hated showing his problems. He also had a zany sense of humour. He took to the computer and MicroWorlds as if they had been part of him since birth. He and his laptop became inseparable. It didn't matter what mathematics topic it was, he wanted to go further and work at it on MicroWorlds. While the class was working on a fractions project, he was testing his understanding of equivalent fractions and adding fractions by producing an animated film in which the fractions moved and transformed into equivalent ones so they could be added. All this was accompanied by flying messages, invented sounds, music, flashing lights and other multimedia paraphernalia. Everything he did went beyond the set task, and he would pose his own problems, always with visual flair. From being a surly, reluctant student, Rob appeared to feel a sense of release with the computer and mathematics when introduced to MicroWorlds.

Cath was a student who excelled at everything and plainly could do more if challenged. The trouble was she never challenged herself. She was always waiting to *be* challenged. Whether it was school that had destroyed the desire to stick her neck out, or an innate personality feature, computers and MicroWorlds broke the spell. Again there was a sense of the computer becoming a best friend against which she could pit her ideas. She had outstanding abilities in language, mathematics and artistic areas, but it was the computer that encouraged her to push herself. She was in Grade 5 and had a sister in Grade 3. Cath took on the role of teaching her sister all the mathematics she was doing in Grade 5. She did this by writing computer software teaching units using the Logo language in MicroWorlds. Area was taught through a set of interactive arrays of small squares that could be operated from the keyboard, and the 'question' and 'answer' interactive quiz facilities (see Figure 4.4) controlled the teaching steps.

Angles of rotation were taught by animation of the angles, then via interaction with teaching question and answer sequences in a similar way. The level of problem-setting was very complex, but Cath set out to solve all the problems she had set herself by experiment, by using the help files and by consulting peers. Only when she got totally stuck for a solution did she approach a teacher who was a bit of an expert, and that happened only once or twice. The resultant teaching units won Cath a prize in the Victorian State Mathematics Talent Quest, and never a more proud recipient stepped on the stage at Melbourne University to receive it.

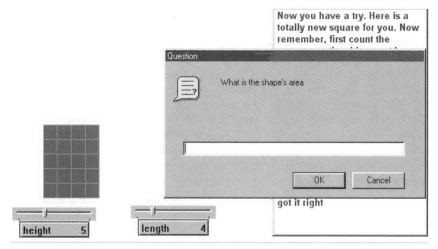

Figure 4.4 A question page in Cath's teaching software for area

Software for mathematics

MicroWorlds is a unique program which has been developed with the sort of problem-setting in mind such as has been described. There are other programs that can allow such outcomes at primary level. MicroWorlds' predecessor, LogoWriter, still has the mathematics embedded in it but without the immediacy of the visual richness. Nevertheless, some researchers recognize the importance of Logo for all learning styles. Lemerise (1992: 198), for instance commented that 'Logo obviously helped at uncovering and supporting different preferential learning styles'. Other multimedia applications can achieve similar objectives, especially if the scripting language used in them can be accessed by older primary children. At lower primary levels, some remarkable results can be achieved with a multimedia word processor such as Textease. Hannah was working with a Grade 3 topic on place value and extending the number system when she discovered that Textease talked back to her with the numbers correctly spoken. For example, if she typed 4593 it spoke back 'four thousand, five hundred, ninety three'. Fascinated, she started investigating how far she could go. We recognize the symptoms already: the non-threatening environment, the spirit of not mattering if we get it wrong, the willingness to dare with a computer. Before long she had produced an illustrated talking chart on the computer for her teacher, moving up to hundreds of millions! Her teacher was somewhat dumbfounded at this, because up to this point she didn't even know that Textease could speak numbers!

The principles of daring and problem-setting described in the children's stories can also be applied to some standard pieces of software in schools.

For example, a class was growing sunflowers as part of a data unit on time. Each child had a 'pet' sunflower and was measuring daily and monitoring against other factors that they had decided beforehand, such as weather and sunlight. As they recorded, they entered the data in a spreadsheet. Mary wanted to know if Excel graphs could have pictures in them. The teacher didn't know and wondered vaguely what Mary had in mind, but Andy knew. He showed Mary how to put picture backgrounds into the graph, and then promptly borrowed the idea and went and found a sunflower picture that he scanned and added as a background (see Figure 4.5).

But Mary had bigger fish to fry. She slipped up to the school library where the digital camera was kept, and each day she brought the camera into the classroom and took a digital picture of her sunflower. The teacher was intrigued because while others copied the idea of taking a picture of their plant, Mary was taking it each day from exactly the same position. At the end of the growing period, she produced a graph like the others with her sunflower on it. But she also copied the graph to MicroWorlds page, made turtle shapes of all her sequence of photographs, and, using the turtles, made a film of the plant growing.

Mainstream word processors and PowerPoint have enough drawing and

Figure 4.5 Andy's sunflower graph in Excel

graphics facilities to allow children to construct remarkable mathematics understandings from the manipulation of the two- and three-dimensional shapes. William was a Microsoft fan, and he always found it difficult to understand why his teacher put so much emphasis on MicroWorlds. While his teacher was encouraging the class to experiment with tessellating shapes in MicroWorlds, William decided to do his in PowerPoint. His animated, all bells and whistles tessellated polygons project, when shown over the class TV monitor, brought the house down. He had done some delving and discovered that he could make some very effective animations in a very simple way and with great impact.

How does it happen?

There are a lot of answers to this question, but perhaps a good starting point is to ask why does it not happen? A teacher at MLC Melbourne (where all students from Grade 5 have their own laptops) is quoted by McDonald (1993): 'You can't put a kid in a classroom with a laptop and expect miracles to happen. The computer itself doesn't do a thing for you. It needs someone to make it happen, someone to give you ideas'. Bigum (1987: 5) points out that 'There is a naive belief among some proponents of educational computing that all that is required to technologically revolutionize schooling is to have technology of the appropriate quality and sophistication in the classroom'.

There are many mathematics classrooms with plenty of computers, or access to sophisticated laboratories and networks where nothing much happens out of the ordinary. So it is obviously not the computers themselves that initiate the deep use of the technology. On the other hand, there obviously do need to be computers. The stories told here testify to the fact that easy access to computers is a necessary requirement. But this does not mean that classrooms full of notebook computers or multiple 'labs' are essential. Small groups with ready access to shared 'pods' of computers can allow daily access. It is the intention to make the best of what we have that is the main need.

The difference is what computers can do to the learning environment if *something* is right. That something can probably best be represented by another story told by Dryden and Vincent (2000: 81–2):

> Mrs A. had taught for many years in various parts of the world, mainly in middle primary years, and was a highly respected 'straight-down-the-line' teacher. In Papert's terms, an 'instructionist'. In Freire's language, 'a banker of knowledge': each child had an account and it had to be filled by the teacher with information.
>
> One year she was persuaded to move from the familiarity of the comfort zone of middle primary into the notebook [computer] programme

in upper primary. Her knowledge of computers was elementary (to put a good gloss on it) and her knowledge of the key software such as Micro-Worlds almost non-existent. She was scared. She knew that many of the children would be far more skilful than she, and she felt she was about to dive into the ocean knowing she couldn't swim. She could have done two things. She could have climbed straight out and continued as though nothing had happened, keeping the computers within a very limited comfort zone. Instead she chose to call for every assistance and swim against the tide. She accepted that she knew nothing and became determined that she would learn alongside the children. She watched what they achieved as they learned from each other and determined to become one of them and learn too, while keeping her hands on and gently guiding the learning framework. Her class was sensational. In a few months the notebook computers had turned her whole teaching philosophy upside down from instructionist to constructionist.

The difference is the willingness of the teacher to allow the children to construct their own meanings, their own problems and their own learning on the computer. Then the teacher has minimum need for language, for 'filling empty accounts', because as long as the teacher knows where they are going, they can sit alongside the children and learn with them. The acceptance by the teacher of a sort of intellectual playfulness in students can be very difficult for some because the sort of mathematics that can emerge from the students can be distinctly 'left of centre'! There is often a judgement to be made concerning at what point to intervene, but in general a quiet word that does not squash the intellectual play is all that is needed. A 10-year-old was using MicroWorlds to make a 'slideshow' of angles, and he had wrapped it up in a rather gory story based on Pokémon characters. The teacher didn't feel the need to intervene because the creativity was so great and the incidental mathematics going on was rich. However, he did make a gentle intervention when, on the last page, a Pokémon beast clawed off the head of a character and the blood poured to the ground when the reader couldn't answer the question about angles correctly!

The letting-go process requires a lot of daring and courage from most of us. It can be very painful. We are giving up our precious belief in the power of language to teach and lead from the front. We are challenging the idea that we as the teachers are the knowledge founts. But the children know far more than us about computers. The teacher still provides the goal, still offers the challenges, but the challenges are only the beginning. There has to be the knowledge of the students that, with the computer in their hands, the challenge is only a minimum and that it is acceptable in this classroom to go further and set greater and greater challenges.

To put the idea on its head for a moment, could Mrs A. have become that sort of teacher without the computer? It is hard not to think that it was the computer that was the catalyst, and it is difficult to think of other possible technologies or literacies that could have caused changes of this nature in her teaching style. Certainly, there have always been exceptional constructivist teachers, but that does not include most of us. Most of us can only be exceptional teachers with a great deal of help. The computer and a piece of constructing software constitutes very powerful help. Seymour Papert has consistently claimed for over 20 years that only the computer can provide the sort of impetus to constructivist-style education environments that previous 'progressive' education movements have frequently tried but almost always failed to achieve. Papert has a different term for constructivism that takes into account the fact that a computer allows children to virtually construct on the screen while learning. He calls it 'constructionism' and he claims that it is built on the assumption that children will do best by finding (fishing) for themselves the specific knowledge they need. The kind of knowledge children most need is the knowledge that will help them gain *more* knowledge. In addition to knowledge about fishing it is as well to have good fishing lines (which is why we need computers) and to know the location of rich waters (which is why we need a large range of mathematically rich activities or 'microworlds') (Papert 1993: 139).

The classroom with one computer and no open-ended software

The issue will continue to arise for a long time that access to computers is too restricted and the correct software is not available to teach in the way described here. At the lowest end of the hardware/software equation it is nearly impossible to work with one computer and poor software provision. However, even when there are substantial computer resources, if creative and open-ended software is missing and there is no learning environment to encourage problem-setting, the sort of outcomes described in the preceding stories does not happen. Often, the mathematics software available in a school controls the child rather than the child being in control of the computer. Thus, even if it has a strong visual element, it fails the creativity test and loses the attention of many of the children. If the idea of mathematical computing is to set a couple of children working on the tables-testing program for part of the numeracy block, then it is difficult to establish the sort of environment needed for experimentation and problem-setting. It does not need a classroom set of laptop computers to establish some sort of creative mathematical environment: two stand-alone computers and some shared laptops would be a start, so that during any class numeracy block, enough computers are available for one of the groups at any one time. Availability of a lab or room of computers, as in some schools, would help, although this immediately limits the group or class by timetabling constraints with other classes.

To return to the beginning – by creating a computing environment for much of our mathematics in primary classes we can establish conditions in which all learning styles can be included in the learning process. Obviously this cannot apply to every part of the mathematics, and MicroWorlds is not the only medium that can be used, but the excitement that comes when the teacher uses such a program and decides to let go and to learn alongside the children is worth the effort. There is more hidden in these stories than just offering opportunities to children with different learning styles. Readers have probably noticed that each time a story is told about a child there is a sense of release from something when the computer and the matching application is introduced. Nathan was not responding to standard school learning environments, but the computer and the software opened a pathway for him to reveal *what was already there but had been hidden*. Amanda was able to respond to a verbal environment but did not reveal her true ability with mathematical problem-solving until the computer and the software allowed her to make mistakes. *The ability had been there but new learning environment allowed her to reveal it.* Rob and Cath used the computer and the learning environment of which it was a part *to escape from the mediocre*. Each story can be viewed from the point of view of releasing what was already there. That is what happens when we tap into learning style preferences, but it also suggests that the learning technologies may be adding a new dimension to learning styles and learning mathematics.

Notes on software

LCSI MicroWorlds is a Canadian product from Logo Computer Systems Incorporated. Their website is www.lcsi.ca. It is worth a visit just to read the constructivist philosophy behind the company.

NRICH Spike Logo is a free Logo product obtainable from www.nrich. maths.org.uk. There are monthly suggestions for its use and problems to solve.

Softease Textease is a British children's multimedia word processor with the ability to speak numbers and limited but very effective mathematical drawing tools.

Broderbund Kidpix is an American children's multimedia program which is being extensively used in parts of Australia to support early years mathematics.

References

Bigum, C. (1987) *Mathematics Curricula Readings*. Geelong: Deakin University Press.

Chiarello, C. (1998) On codes of meaning and the meaning of codes, in M. Beeman and C. Chiarello (eds) *Right Hemisphere Language Comprehension*, pp. 141–60. Mawah, NJ: Erlbaum.

Costa, S. (2000) You want every year five student to have her own laptop?, in J. Little and B. Dixon (eds) *Transforming Learning – An Anthology of Miracles in Technology Rich Classrooms*, pp. 67–76. Port Melbourne: Kids Technology Foundation.

Dixon, J. (1983) *The Spatial Child*. Springfield, IL: Thomas.

Dryden, J. and Vincent, J. (2000) A tool for all learning styles, in J. Little and B. Dixon (eds) *Transforming Learning – An Anthology of Miracles in Technology Rich Classrooms*, pp. 77–84. Port Melbourne: Kids Technology Foundation.

Gazzaniga, M. (1998) The split brain re-visited, *Scientific American*, July: 34–9.

Goldenberg, E. (1995) Ruminations about dynamic imagery (and a strong plea for research), in R. Sutherland and J. Mason (eds) *Exploring Mental Imagery with Computers in Mathematics Education*, NATO Advanced Science Institute Series. Berlin: Springer-Verlag.

Goldenberg, E., Cuoco, A. and Mark, J. (1998) A role for geometry in general education, in R. Lehrer and D. Chazan (eds) *Designing Learning Environments for Developing Understanding of Geometry and Space*, pp. 3–44. Mawah, NJ: Erlbaum.

Goody, J. (1977) *The Domestication of the Savage Mind*. New York: Cambridge University Press.

Harel, I. and Papert, S. (1991) Software design as a learning environment, in I. Harel and S. Papert (eds) *Constructionism*, pp. 41–84. Norwood, NJ: Ablex.

Kaput, J. (2000) Implications of the shift from isolated, expensive technology to connected, inexpensive, diverse and ubiquitous technologies, *Proceedings*, *Technology in Mathematics Education Conference*, Auckland, University of Auckland and Auckland University of Technology.

Lemerise, T. (1992) On intra- and interindividual differences in children's learning styles, in C. Hoyles and R. Noss (eds) *Learning Mathematics and Logo*, pp. 191–221. Cambridge, MA: MIT Press.

McDonald, H. (1993) Teacher change: philosophy and technology, *Australian Educational Computing*, 8.

Ornstein, R. (1997) *The Right Mind*. Orlando, FL: Harcourt Brace.

Papert, S. (1993) *The Children's Machine*. New York: Basic Books.

Riding, R. and Raynor, S. (1998) *Cognitive Styles and Learning Strategies*. London: David Fulton.

Sfard, A. and Leron, U. (1996) Just give me a computer and I will move the earth: programming as a catalyst of a cultural revolution in the mathematics classroom, *International Journal of Computers for Mathematical Learning*, 1: 189–95.

Sinatra, R. (1986) *Visual Literacy Connections to Thinking, Reading and Writing*. Springfield, IL: Thomas.

Vincent, J. (2000) Personal notebook computers, visually talented children and mathematics, *Papers from IMECT2*. www.nrich.maths.org.uk/conference/imect2

5

TEACHING THE COMPUTER

Ronnie Goldstein and David Pratt

Introduction

The usual expectation when computers are used in school is that the children who are using them will be learning rather than teaching. Also, teaching is a process not normally considered in terms of the benefits to the teacher. So the process of teaching the computer is not one that is emphasized very often. But we think that it is actually a valuable learning process that can easily occur in school and that, if you are aware of the phenomenon it is likely to become more common in your classroom.

When children write a procedure in Logo they might type 'to square' with the intention of teaching the machine a new word, 'square', which it did not know before. The word 'to' is used in the Logo language precisely because the user is teaching the computer 'to' draw a square. The result of the new procedure is that when anyone subsequently types the word 'square' the computer does precisely what the writer of the procedure taught it to do. When a child devises their own spreadsheet (rather than using one that has been produced by someone else), the child is entering formulae into the spreadsheet and teaching the computer which calculations will be done when the spreadsheet is used at a subsequent time. In

Pathways,[1] the game that can be played at the computer is defined entirely by the rules that were entered by the children when they taught the machine how to play their game.

When children use a computer they are often answering questions that the software or the teacher has posed. When children are teaching the computer, however, they will be making several of their own decisions about the direction of their work and how they are to achieve their aims. Children might start their work with Logo by typing commands directly into the computer, but as soon as they use procedures they are *teaching* the computer. When children are using a spreadsheet template and simply entering data to observe the results, they are using the software without teaching the computer. Teaching the spreadsheet, on the other hand, implies that the children are writing formulae and devising the actual sheet. Pathways was designed to allow children to design their own games, with the result that teaching the computer happens for most of the time.

Every teacher knows that one of the best ways to understand something is to teach it to someone else. But teaching a computer is not exactly the same as teaching other people. People have a way of interpreting what is being said to them. They read the gestures and the facial expressions of their teachers as well as the words that are spoken. The intonation of the voice is important and matters judged to be obvious are not always articulated. All this may generally assist the learning process, but what matters here is that computers are essentially stupid so they cannot interpret any of the commands they are given and the teacher has to articulate everything that is to be learned. A computer has no knowledge of what its programmer is attempting to do. It only knows what it has been told and so the children who are teaching it are compelled to use precise, unambiguous and formal language. The children respect this requirement because they understand that it is not an arbitrary imposition (as many of those made by teachers often are). In today's world we cannot yet address machines informally by the spoken word and, mathematically at least, there may be fewer benefits when we can.

There are other characteristics of computers that make them valuable objects to teach. One of these is their interactivity. Without any computers we might use paper and pencil, which are useful devices for recording results but less valuable for experimental purposes because they do not encourage an exploratory approach or suggest activity. The computer, in contrast, begs to be used. It always feels quite appropriate to key in ideas and try them out. In fact, children are usually so willing to explore different possibilities that teachers are more likely to have the reverse problem of having to persuade them to stand back and reflect occasionally.

Another feature of computers that makes them ideal to teach is their fast and reliable feedback. Some software today, which boasts continual feedback, actually just tells the user whether the input was 'right' or 'wrong', saying nothing about the nature of what was typed. When a procedure has been written in Logo, however, the child naturally wants to test it by running the procedure, and the computer then informs the child, immediately and reliably, what the actual effects of the procedure are. The feedback obtained in this way is qualitative. It informs the user about the input. Similarly, a spreadsheet and Pathways may not do what was *intended* by their programmer, but they will always do precisely what they have been taught to do and they will provide their feedback very quickly. The computer is not as threatening to teach as a human pupil might be, because it has no expectations of its teacher. It does not anticipate how its programmer will work. In particular there are never expected responses that need to be entered before progress is permitted and there are never time constraints that have been imposed. With Logo, with spreadsheets and with Pathways, the children can be assured that the computer will exercise infinite patience while they discuss what to type next.

In the National Curriculum in England and Wales (DfEE 2000), the communication of mathematics is recognized as one of three main strands in 'Using and Applying Mathematics'. For example, in the case of 'Using and Applying Number at Key Stage 2' (upper primary school), on page 21 it states that teachers are expected to introduce the children to the following ideas and skills:

- use notation diagrams and symbols correctly within a given problem;
- present and interpret solutions in the context of the problem;
- communicate mathematically, including the use of precise mathematical language.

We believe that teaching the computer is a particularly good strategy for teaching aspects of communication as represented in the National Curriculum. Below we discuss two main aspects of teaching the computer. The section entitled 'Formalizing' describes the mathematical processes in which the children are involved and 'What is the purpose?' considers more general benefits.

Formalizing

When we do mathematics, we express our ideas in a special language, and this process involves formalizing. We express our ideas in mathematics so that they become accessible for manipulation using the rules of mathematics and, out of that manipulation, new results or ideas may emerge. Also, the ideas are expressed less ambiguously, enabling rigorous scrutiny and discussion. When we teach the computer, we do not express our ideas in conventional mathematical language. We need to express ourselves in Logo, in a spreadsheet or in Pathways and the process is generally motivated by the need to obtain results, sometimes graphical and sometimes numerical, that can be observed on the computer. The language we use in any of these situations is likely to have some mathematical attributes.

When a mathematician finds a pattern of some sort that can be used to predict further results, he or she is conjecturing. The process of doing mathematics involves making a conjecture or hypothesis, testing it and amending it. There are clear parallels between this process and that of teaching a machine. To write a procedure in Logo is equivalent to making a conjecture; when the procedure is run and its effects are observed the conjecture is being tested; and when all is not well, to debug the procedure and edit it are equivalent to amending the conjecture. Similar statements to the previous one could be made for devising a new column for a spreadsheet or generating a rule for an object in Pathways. Below, we examine closely some examples of children using different software to teach the computer. Our aim is to elaborate on the formalizing process in which the children were engaged.

Teaching the computer to draw a house

When children use Logo, a natural activity is to draw a picture. It scarcely matters which picture they choose since, by and large, the children will need to use the same sorts of programming structures. Here we describe two children who drew a house, a familiar activity to those who have observed Logo being used. They had typed in various commands and, through a process of trial and improvement, they had gradually managed to make the turtle draw the outline of the house they wanted. It was an open pentagon shape (see Figure 5.1). They knew that they could teach the computer to draw their house shape automatically by writing a procedure, and then they would easily be able to make changes to that procedure and use it several times, perhaps to create a street of houses.

Figure 5.1   A house shape drawn in Logo

They inspected what they had already typed and they tidied up their work to teach the computer the following procedure:

```
to house
fd 50
rt 45
fd 50
rt 90
fd 50
rt 45
fd 50
end
```

To achieve this working procedure and teach the machine effectively, the two children needed to use their turtle to draw a shape. This meant that they needed to link two different perspectives: that of the drawing and that of the formal language of Logo.

Teaching the computer a wallpaper pattern

Daniel and Anthony, aged 11, were at a more advanced stage and they used their turtle to create a wallpaper pattern on the screen (see Figure 5.2). They wrote just three procedures – z, x and s – and their Logo code was

Figure 5.2 Daniel and Anthony's wallpaper design

very highly structured and succinct. The procedure z draws the motif once and moves the turtle on ready to draw the next one:

```
to z
repeat 9 [fd 30 lt 160]
pu fd 45 pd
end
```

The procedure x produces a single row of stars by repeating z ten times and then moving the turtle to the start of the next row:

```
to x
repeat 10 [z]
pu bk 450 rt 90 fd 45 lt 90 pd
end
```

The main 'super procedure' that has to be typed to activate the drawing is s and this serves to clear the screen, place the turtle at the correct starting position and then repeat x six times to draw the six rows:

```
to s
cs
pu setpos [−300 160] rt 90 pd
repeat 6 [x]
end
```

If the children know from the start that they want to repeat a design on the screen several times, they are bound to look for a structured approach which is more efficient than a linear string of commands. However, this is not an easy task and most of the children in the group produced code which occupied several pages and which was far less structured than Daniel and Anthony's. Appreciating this new perspective, one that places emphasis on structure, is the hallmark of formalizing and also underlies the following examples, which are based on the use of spreadsheets and Pathways.

Teaching the computer the dimensions of a sheep pen

Jordan and Stelios, aged 11, were using a spreadsheet to solve the problem depicted in Figure 5.3. Janet Ainley (1996) gives a detailed account of Jordan and Stelios' progress on this problem but here we pick out some of the elements that focus on formalizing. The boys began by using straws to make sheep pens and they held the straws against a ruler, which acted as the wall. They measured the length and the width of their straw shape (see Figure 5.4) and entered the data into two cells of their spreadsheet (see Figure 5.5). (The class had several computers available to them and they had often worked with spreadsheets.)

A farmer has 30m of flexible fencing.
She wants to make a rectangular pen for
her sheep against a stone wall.

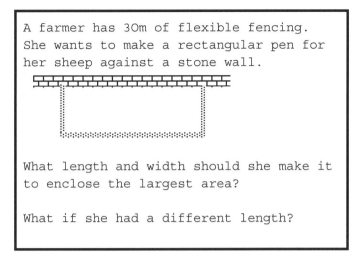

What length and width should she make it
to enclose the largest area?

What if she had a different length?

Figure 5.3   The sheep pen activity

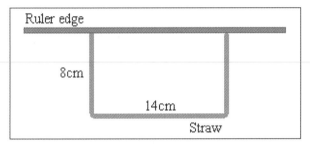

Figure 5.4   The first rectangle, made from straws

	A	B
1	**Width**	**Length**
2	8	14

Figure 5.5   The start of Jordan and Stelios' spreadsheet

Jordan and Stelios repeated this process for several different arbitrarily chosen rectangles. Their teacher helped them to write a formula for cell C2 (=A2*B2) and then to copy it for all the rows of their sheet so that the computer evaluated the area of each sheep pen (see Figure 5.6). The boys wanted to use the graphing facility to see if it would help them to identify the largest sheep pen but they did not have enough data for their graph to make any sense. They entered a few more rows into their spreadsheet

	A	B	C
1	**Width**	**Length**	**Area**
2	8	14	112
3	5	20	100
4	2	26	52

Figure 5.6   The spreadsheet evaluated the area of each sheep pen

manually and, after a while, they began to enter lengths and widths without actually using the straws to make any pens. Apparently, they had developed a mental method for calculating the length of the pen from any given width and so it was not necessary for them to continue with the straws. It turned out that they were doubling the width of the pen and then, to calculate the length, they were working out how much needed to be added onto that answer to get a total of 30.

The boys' teacher took the opportunity to suggest that if they had a method of working out the length of the pen, they should be able to teach this method to the computer. Jordan and Stelios were aware that, once the computer knew such a method, it would be possible to generate lots of results very quickly simply by 'filling down' (i.e. copying the formula to all the rows of the spreadsheet). The first two rows of the spreadsheet that Jordan and Stelios finally designed are shown in Figure 5.7. The formula in cell B2 means that when the width is 8 the correct length, 14, automatically appears in that cell. However, it was not easy for the boys to shift their perspective and formalize their mental method to achieve this result.

Jordan and Stelios had talked informally about 'doubling the width' and there was some initial confusion about the need to write 2 * A2 in their formula. The major hurdle, however, was how to teach the computer to keep adding numbers onto that answer until 30 was reached. At one point, Jordan commented: 'We need to tell it like, we want to tell that there's 30 over there, if we times, say it was five, times by two it becomes ten, and

	A	B	C
1	**Width**	**Length**	**Area**
2	8	=30 - 2 * A2	=A2 * B2

Figure 5.7   The first two rows of the final spreadsheet

what, and tell it to know how much is left on the ruler.' When asked to elaborate, Jordan simply said: 'I know that ten add twenty is thirty.'

There is no direct equivalent to their informal method of adding on that can be applied in the spreadsheet. Jordan and Stelios worked on this problem for some considerable time before their teacher intervened. She eventually suggested starting with the length of fencing and cutting off the two widths. Jordan replied: 'If we start with thirty, take away that cell times two.'

Their initial informal method of calculation mirrored the practical method of choosing the width, bending the straw at both ends and measuring the length of straw left between the two folds. But the boys' teacher had suggested a new focus – to start with 30 and subtract the widths. This new focus was much closer to the mathematical language required by the spreadsheet. The result of the intervention was dramatic, with Jordan and Stelios quickly seeing how they needed to change their formula. They went on to generate many results and they found the 'best' pen by examining the data and the graph.

The shift of perspective was successfully achieved because the boys' initial exploration had cleared the ground by making partial progress (e.g. in sorting out doubling) and they saw the need for an alternative formulation that the spreadsheet would understand. Also, their teacher was able to find a perspective that was meaningful in terms of the practical work but which translated more easily into the spreadsheet's mathematical language. The spreadsheet then acted as a laboratory to try out initial ideas, gain feedback and appreciate what worked and what did not. It was also a very strong source of motivation because it was clearly a productive activity to teach the computer.

Teaching the computer a video game

For our third example, we focus on Harry and Laura, aged 7, who were using Pathways to develop their Dome game (see Figure 5.8). Pathways is a formal language where the children use icons to generate their rules and these rules, created by the children, define the game that is being built. In Harry and Laura's game, one player controlled the clown with the joystick while a second player controlled the shark with the mouse. There were also some turtles in their game (new objects can be created as required) and these had been instructed to move automatically and randomly around the screen.

Pathways is designed so that the children can switch to playing their game as and when they need to do so and, in the Dome game, the players competed to collect the spikes from the roof of the Millennium Dome before the turtles exploded them.

Harry and Laura had just programmed one of the spikes and they had given it two rules (see Figure 5.9). The first rule instructed the spike to be

Figure 5.8   Harry and Laura's Dome game

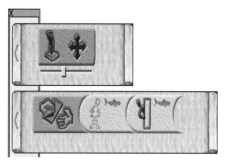

Figure 5.9   The rules given to one of the spikes

driven by the joystick, in all directions; and the second rule told the shark that, when it received a message, it should hide and then show itself. In Pathways all the rules are enacted repeatedly and so this made the shark flash.

   The first of these rules is a straightforward instruction, whereas the second is conditional: the shark only flashed when it received a message. When working with children using Pathways we felt that thinking in terms of conditional statements was sometimes obvious, but there were also occasions when they preferred to think narratively. When Harry was asked

Figure 5.10 Eleanor's game

what the second rule meant, he replied with a conditional statement: 'When the spike sends the message, I hide and then I . . .' When Laura was asked what happened in the game she used narrative language to describe the action: 'It will hide, then it will show it, then it will hide, then it will show it.' Both responses were appropriate since they were answering different questions. One question was about the rule, while the other was about the game. We see these as two different perspectives.

Some children do not find the change of perspective so easy. Eleanor's (age 7) entire game (see Figure 5.10) was more like a story in which the cat pushed the meat (with its bottom!) towards the dog. When the dog and the meat came into contact, the meat disappeared (it was eaten by the dog), a sound was made and the cat moved away.

Eleanor wanted the dog to eat the meat and we expected that she might come up with a rule for the dog such as 'When I touch the meat, I hide the meat'. We found, however, that Eleanor preferred to use a narrative account. When asked specifically about the rule that was needed, she responded: 'I want it to say that the cat goes over to the meat before the dog, and the cat picks up the meat and pushes it along to the dog and then the dog eats it and then they just run round the street.'

Did Eleanor want to write a narrative story that would always be identical on the screen and where the 'player' had no active role? Or did she envisage the same sort of game that we had in mind, where the player had the freedom to move the cat and push the meat anywhere on the screen so that the meat would only disappear when it touched the dog? We can only speculate. A few minutes later, Eleanor did use the appropriate icons for a conditional structure. She gradually became more fluent in expressing rules through conditional language so that, later, when she wanted her cat to move, she suggested: 'Maybe we could have when I am touching an object, I move forward 30.'

Let us examine more closely the narrative and conditional perspectives by considering the following invented situation. Imagine a scenario where you could pick up a hammer and move it across the screen. If you were to observe that the hammer moves across the screen, touches the gong and a sound is played, you might use narrative language and relate the story as: 'I moved the hammer across the screen then it touched the gong and then there was a sound.'

Now imagine that you are programming the computer to display this effect in Pathways as a game. If your program were to follow the narrative statement above, there would be no game to play, just a sequence of actions on the screen which could not be affected by any player. To implement a player-controlled game in Pathways you would need to teach the hammer a rule such as 'When I am touching the gong, I make a sound'. The perspective of the programmer of games is quite different from that of the observer or player of games, as it involves adopting a different language – one that places emphasis on conditionals. We see the linking of these perspectives as an essential aspect of formalizing in Pathways.

Although the language in Pathways is iconic rather than symbolic (as in Logo and spreadsheets), the shift of perspective in teaching the computer nevertheless demands the use of new language. In Logo and in a spreadsheet the symbolic language is more recognizable as mathematical but, in all three cases, the adoption of the new language requires the use of a formal and precise code with the express purpose of building a product, defined through that language, which becomes available to general scrutiny.

What is the purpose?

Writing algorithms

An algorithm is a method or a step-by-step process that works in general. There is, for example, a standard written algorithm for adding two numbers. Figure 5.11 shows the working of a person who is part of the way through using this standard algorithm. This algorithm is 'standard' because it works for any decimal numbers and it also works however many numbers there are to be added together. When children teach their computer to perform algorithms, the computer provides 'purpose' – it

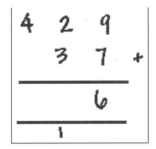

Figure 5.11 Working through the standard algorithm for addition

generates a reason for the children to be absolutely precise and not to allow any fuzzy thinking.

School mathematics syllabuses are full of standard algorithms that need to be learned and used productively. But it is important, in our view, that children also write their own algorithms occasionally. Not only will this provide a very full understanding of the subject matter in hand but teaching the computer to perform the algorithm provides a real purpose for the children.

When Logo is used to draw a square the child may be considered to be using an algorithmic or procedural definition of the square (move forwards and turn right 90 degrees, four times), rather than the more common definition (four equal sides and four equal angles) that relies on certain properties. And when a child learns this procedural definition to achieve a square on the screen they have certainly improved their understanding of what a square is. It is worth noting at this stage that the procedural or algorithmic definition of the square is more tangible, more concrete than the abstract formal definition. It is easier to understand because it describes what needs to be done to actually make the square.

Consider now a class in Year 5 where the teacher expected many of her pupils to be able to understand that for any two numbers, the mean average is half of their sum. She started by building on the children's intuitive ideas. There was a class discussion and, when the teacher asked who knew the word 'average', none of the children had a clear idea but the word 'middle' did crop up once or twice. The teacher drew a simple number line and stressed that the mean average is the number on the line at the midpoint between the two numbers in question (see Figure 5.12).

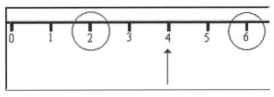

Figure 5.12 The mean of the two numbers, 2 and 6, is the middle number, 4

This was then followed by some informal activities, which helped to develop the children's intuitive ideas. The methods of evaluating the mean varied from pupil to pupil. For instance, for the numbers 3 and 9, some children drew their own number line and picked out the middle number by observation. Others subtracted the numbers (9 − 3 = 6) and added half the difference (3) to the lower number of the pair. Some children added the numbers in the original pair (3 + 9= 12) and understood that the mean had to be half of this sum.

It was the teacher's aim to develop the formal definition and this was achieved by using a spreadsheet and getting the children to teach the computer to evaluate the result. In order to generate purpose for the children, the teacher told them that they would be developing a spreadsheet that might subsequently be used by younger children in the school who could not work out the answers for themselves. Although the spreadsheet was never likely to be used in this way, the idea of writing some software for others was very appealing and motivating for all concerned. Expressing the algorithm verbally would have allowed the children to be less precise in their thinking, and writing it on paper would have had no real purpose for them.

The final result that the teacher had in mind was for the children to have two cells in which the original numbers were to be placed and a third cell where the mean average was to be calculated (see Figure 5.13). The simplicity of this final result does not describe all the detail of the children's discussions and arguments as they tried to establish the formula for the algorithm they wanted the spreadsheet to perform. The major shift for most of the children was that, in order to teach the computer, they needed a mathematical formula and their visual approach of observing the number line was not sufficient. Further to this the computer needed to be taught a single method that always worked, no matter which two numbers were placed in cells A1 and B1. Some children started with an idea that was relatively simple, intuitively. They wanted to add half the difference between the two numbers to the smaller number. But this was not at all straightforward to teach the computer. There were many steps in this algorithm and the problem that defeated those who started this way was the difficulty of telling the computer which of the numbers was the smaller. The teacher was also aware that the children's intuitive methods did not necessarily work when there were more than two numbers. The

	A	B	C
1	**First number**	**Second number**	**Mean average**
2			$=(A2+B2)/2$

Figure 5.13 The teacher's intended outcome

mean of three numbers cannot be found by considering any 'middle' number, whereas the formula the children needed to develop could be generalized to deal with any number of numbers.

The child's perspective

So much of the mathematics that children do in school lacks any real purpose for them. Children are usually directed by their teacher, their workbook or by the software that they happen to be using. Teachers need to consider the National Curriculum when they decide what to teach but there is rarely any stimulus to look further and think about the context for the work. It is often assumed, therefore, that the child's purpose will be identical to the teacher's, but it is rarely the case that the mathematics curriculum itself will provide sufficient motivation for our pupils. Teaching the computer provides a context in which the children work, but this may not be entirely free of its own problems. Young children may not yet be able to distinguish clearly between the game in their heads and the one that they want to create on the screen.

Working with Pathways is all about teaching the computer and we are keen for the children to have full control of the games they design. Before children start to use the computer we tell them that the game is to be theirs and so their imaginations run riot. Of course the games they want to design are usually based on recent experiences or on video-games they have played before. When Laura and Harry were about to start, Laura said she would like to create a Millennium Dome game. It became clear after further discussion that Laura had recently visited the Dome. She could imagine a game in which the aim was to collect the spikes from the top of the Dome and transfer them to certain zones. The imagined game went further into fantasy as they suggested that their characters (i.e. the ones they controlled) might be a dog for Laura and a fish for Harry. As they progressed, Laura and Harry obviously learned many things about Pathways and what they might be able to achieve using the software. We had written a simple game to start them off and they had begun by changing the rules for the dog. This bottom-up approach was not inappropriate but, even after working with some of the rules for more than one session, their fantasized game still had a lot of meaning. Harry had been immersed in a discussion with Laura about certain rules and which objects should own those rules when suddenly he surprised us by saying, 'Because that big spike . . . I wonder what would happen if we get all the spikes? I wonder if the game will actually finish?'

In fact, Harry then said that the game might automatically stop when all the spikes had exploded despite no rule having being written to that effect. The imagined game seemed to interpose with the game being built. An appropriate ending for the Dome game could, indeed, have been when all the spikes were exploded and Harry talked as if this might happen automatically. Was Harry just articulating this imagined ending, was he assuming that the initial game he and Laura had been given contained this ending, or did he really think this could happen without his instruction?

At a still later stage, their thinking about the game seemed to be entirely governed by the rules that were to be given to the objects of the game. Harry and Laura were discussing how their game might progress and the phrases they were using were close in their form to the rules as they would have been expressed by the software. (The children often used the software's facility to 'speak' the rules.) They seemed to have developed a clear appreciation of the relationship between the game inside their heads and the rules that they would need to teach the computer. But the facility to talk in terms of the formal rules of the software does not develop so fast in all young children and there does not always seem to be a clear-cut distinction between what they want to happen and what will happen. At some points the children's thinking is dominated by their fantasies. At other times they are constrained by the computer and what they can achieve using the tools of Pathways. It may be that some children who are not so comfortable with formal rules prefer to spend more of their time in their fantasies. We have seen children play their computer games with many rules that are still only inside their heads. We do, however, expect a transition so that, as time progresses, the computer's demands become more dominant.

The software

If children are to enjoy full control of their activities, the software they use is critical. There is plenty of software available that provides exercises for the students and where the whole concept of teaching the computer can be exploited. But even with Logo, spreadsheets and Pathways there are differences that may be useful to note. These differences concern what we call the 'width' and the 'height' of the software.

The width concerns the number of possible avenues that might be explored by the children. Logo is very wide because, after they have drawn some simple pictures, there are many different challenges open to them. For instance, children might draw patterns or pictures such as a keyboard or a wallpaper design that are of a repetitive nature. They might simulate movement by repeatedly erasing a drawing and replacing it in a new position. Or they might write a quiz where the computer has to respond to inputs from the user of the program.

Spreadsheets are more limited than Logo because, as far as teaching the computer is concerned, they are primarily about numbers. However, many numerical situations can be tackled effectively through the use of a spreadsheet.

It is difficult for us to be clear about the width of Pathways because the software is new and is still being developed. However, it seems that the limitations on width are more severe than those of Logo. Children are limited to a game or a simple narrative story that unfolds. Certain types of games are difficult or impossible to teach to the computer. For example, board games based on a rectangular grid are not impossible but would be very hard for a young child to program, at least in the current version of Pathways.

The height of the software refers to what might in time be achieved, both in terms of the programming and the mathematics. Logo is a powerful computer language which has few limitations in these respects, and spreadsheets are also very powerful. But, again, we are uncertain about the potential of Pathways. One plan for its development is that the child can access the underlying language, Imagine[2], while still inside Pathways. This would increase dramatically the height and the width of the software, provided the language itself was not too difficult for them.

Teaching the computer often places substantial control in the hands of the children. When children have this degree of control they will want to exercise it by following up their ideas, which are often quite idiosyncratic. The less restricted the software in terms of width and height, the more empowered are the children to follow through their ideas.

The teacher's perspective

When children are teaching the computer the context may be clear. The children may be working at the computer in order to produce a game or some other activity for their peers to enjoy. Of course, when the originators' activities are completed, others may give the software little attention but, nevertheless, the motivation is there for the creators of the software. Giving simple directions to others is often a satisfying process and we have seen university students motivated entirely through the process of writing web pages to be read by other students.

There will be additional advantages if teachers can suggest activities in which the children see some direct benefit for themselves. For instance, Jordan and Stelios had entered some data for a few sheep pens manually and when they graphed their results they quickly understood that they needed more data for the graphs to become meaningful. Teaching the computer the correct formula meant that many more rows could be generated in their spreadsheet, thus producing the data they needed.

So how much do teachers need to prepare when children are about to teach the computer? In the early stages, children need very little support to develop ideas in Logo or in Pathways and so they can, quite reasonably, be stimulated entirely by the software. Of course, assistance will be required as they are working but it is unnecessary for the teacher to spend a long time preparing particular lessons. (There will, of course, be times at a later stage when children encounter more difficult ideas and need some explicit teaching.) In Logo, children will engage in teaching the computer how to draw a picture or create some dynamic effect. The teacher can be confident that, even though the context is not necessarily explicitly mathematical, the children will be working with important mathematical ideas such as distance, angle or variable. In Pathways, the children will easily engage in building a game. Again the context is not obviously mathematical and yet the children will need to use conditional thinking in order to build their game. A spreadsheet, however, does not itself suggest any particular activity for the children and so, when it is to be used for teaching the computer, the teacher has to find an appropriate activity. It takes careful planning to find an activity that children want to explore and which also leads to an appreciation of a mathematical concept.

Conclusion

In this chapter we have argued that teaching the computer is a particularly powerful strategy for learning mathematics. We can summarize by reiterating the main aspects that we have elaborated above:

- Teaching is a constructive way to learn.
- A central mathematical utility when teaching the computer is formalizing, and this becomes a meaningful process in the context of designing software for others to use.
- A feature of the formalizing process is a shift in perspective; the precise nature of the shift depends upon the activity.
- Another feature of formalizing is that children have to adopt a more precise and general type of language such as that employed in standard algorithms. Conventionally such algorithms are often seen as meaningless but teaching the algorithm to a computer can become a purposeful challenge.
- When the child teaches the computer, the fast, reliable and qualitative feedback helps them to be in control and this is often beneficial in terms of motivation.
- If the child is going to be able to take ownership, the software and the activity based upon that software need to be sufficiently open to encourage creativity.
- The activity needs to be not only purposeful but well designed so that, in pursuing their purpose, the child is likely to encounter powerful mathematical ideas.

We wish to end by discussing the extent to which teaching the computer is essentially and necessarily a mathematical process. We believe that teaching the turtle in Logo and teaching the spreadsheet are clearly processes of formalizing fuzzy ideas into a precise language that the machine can understand, and that communicating with the machine in these cases involves a quasi-mathematical language akin to doing algebra. Furthermore, it is not difficult to recognize aspects of this process that are similar to modelling, which is recognized as a fundamental part of applied mathematics (we discuss the idea that the use of Pathways is a form of modelling in Goldstein and Pratt 2001).

However, there is today plenty of non-mathematical software available in which the players are teaching the computer. We see many products on the market in which the child controls the machine. Simulations such as Sim City and Theme Park[3] (and many others) allow the child to make fundamental decisions about the way the simulation should progress. We acknowledge that there are powerful educational opportunities in the use of such software, but is the process mathematical? For us, the answer hangs on the issue of formalizing, which we see as the critical aspect of the relationship between teaching the computer and mathematics. Formalizing depends on a translation from an everyday type of language to a conventional and precise one, where there is a particularly high degree of rigour and shared meaning.

In this respect, we see a difference between the use of Logo or spreadsheets and the use of Sim City type simulations. Where does that leave Pathways? Is the use of Pathways mathematical? Pathways has some of the aspects of Sim City in that it is controlled by direct manipulation rather than through the use of symbols or text. However, although the language is iconic, it has the properties of precision and, like any language, its building blocks are capable of combination in different ways that infer different meanings. (For a more detailed discussion of the relationship between the children's ideas for a game and its formalization in Pathways, see Goldstein *et al.* 2001.) Pathways is, of course, far more restricted than Logo or spreadsheets and some of this restriction occurs precisely because of its iconic nature. Indeed, the opportunities for generalizing are few because of the lack of named variables. Nevertheless, when children use Pathways to teach the computer they are formalizing in a way that makes us believe that their activity has a strong mathematical element.

Notes

1 Pathways is being developed as part of the Playground project, EU ESE Project #29329 (see www.ioe.ac.uk/playground). In the Playground project, a team of researchers and developers from several countries is exploring how young children (6 to 8 years) construct their own computer-based games.
2 Imagine, a new 32-bit version of Logo soon to be available from Logotron, is an innovative modern programming environment especially designed for children to explore and develop. It is a powerful tool for designing open visual applications.
3 Both Sim City and Theme Park are distributed by Electronic Arts Ltd and published by Bullfrog Production Ltd. See: www.ea.com/

References

Ainley, J. (1996) Purposeful contexts for formal notation in a spreadsheet environment, *Journal of Mathematical Behaviour*, 15(4): 405–22.

DfEE (Department for Education and Employment) (2000) *The National Curriculum for England and Wales: Mathematics*. London: DfEE.

Goldstein, R. and Pratt, D. (2001) Michael's computer game: a case of open modelling, *Proceedings of the Twenty-Fifth Annual Conference of the International Group for the Psychology of Mathematics Education*. Utrecht: Utrecht University.

Goldstein, R., Noss, R., Kalas, I. and Pratt, D. (2001) Building rules, in M. Beynon, C.L. Nehaniv and K. Dautenhahn (eds) *Proceedings of the 4th International Conference of Cognitive Technology*, CT2001, pp. 267–81. Coventry: University of Warwick.

6

EXPANDING HORIZONS: THE POTENTIAL OF THE INTERNET TO ENHANCE LEARNING

Jenni Way and Toni Beardon

Introduction

The Internet is now part of our lives and is becoming increasingly important in our day-to-day functions in work, education and leisure. Indeed, to be a citizen in the 'global information society' now requires 'web literacy'. In a growing number of nations, including the UK, the USA, Australia and Canada, almost all primary-school children (aged 5 to 12 years) are beginning to learn about, and to acquire, the basic skills needed to access and use the Internet. Many also learn how to make productive use of the Internet to enhance and support their learning experiences at school across a range of subject areas. These children are being introduced to the enormous potential of the Internet to enhance their learning and are being empowered to embark on a journey of lifelong learning. Is not the purpose of education to expand horizons for our students?

With the number of households connected to the Internet in developed countries climbing to over 50 per cent, many children are also supplementing their school-based education at home by utilizing resources available from websites. Distance education is a fast-growing form of learning that takes advantage of the information delivery and communication functions of the Internet. The Internet as an educational medium and resource is now firmly entrenched and it is rapidly becoming a serious educational disadvantage to be without access to the Internet, giving rise to the notion of the 'digital divide'.

Many websites designed to support mathematics education for school-aged students have emerged in recent years. They have been designed by a wide variety of people and organizations for a range of audiences and to serve diverse purposes. Some are like electronic reference books and range from small, discrete pieces of information to encyclopedic capacity. Others offer opportunities that go far beyond what passive text can provide and take advantage of the characteristics of the Internet that distinguish it from printed material and even computer software. These characteristics include global interaction and communication with peers and mentors, dynamic information access and far-reaching independent research potential. The Internet offers users exciting learning opportunities and access to people and information never before possible for the 'average' person. With a vast array of mathematics-related websites already 'out there', and more coming online each week, teachers and educators need an approach for locating and selecting suitable ones.

This chapter features a well-established and respected mathematics education website, based in the UK, to illustrate the powerful potential for learning offered by the Internet to children and to the adults who guide their learning.

Children on the Internet

The Computer Economics company expects the number of Internet-using minors worldwide to surpass 77 million by the year 2005, with the most rapid growth in North America and the Asian Pacific (see Table 6.1).

In the UK, 65 per cent of all children in the 7 to 16 age range (4.8 million) use the Internet. The most common use among children at home is for doing homework (56 per cent), followed by sending email (43 per cent)

Table 6.1   Projected growth in Internet users under 18 years

Area	2001 (millions)	2005 (millions)
Africa	0.09	0.36
Asian Pacific	5.21	22.23
Europe	6.17	15.34
Middle East	0.16	0.43
North America	13.71	36.92
South America	0.48	1.78
Total worldwide	**25.82**	**77.06**

Source: Adapted from Computer Economics website, 22 April 1999

and playing games (42 per cent). Most of these children (81 per cent) have access to the web in school, while 62 per cent have access from home. (NOP Research Group 2000).

In Australia, 95 per cent of children aged 5 to 14 have used a computer and 47 per cent have accessed the Internet in the past 12 months. Of Australian households, 34 per cent are connected to the Internet. At home, children tend to use the Internet for learning purposes and school-related activities, as well as a source of games. Email and chatrooms were also utilized by this age group (Australian Bureau of Statistics 2000).

In the USA, a survey conducted in 2000 reported the Internet to be a positive force in children's education, with more than 40 per cent of 9–17-year-old schoolchildren saying it had improved their attitude to attending school. Almost half the children accessing the Internet at home in the USA do so for schoolwork. Parents also reported that Internet use tends to reduce a child's television watching time, but does not reduce other activities such as reading and playing outdoors (National School Boards Foundation 2000).

In February 1999, about 88 per cent of Canadian elementary schools were connected to the Internet and about one third of the students had used email. About the same proportion had already disseminated information via the Internet or participated in the production or maintenance of a website. A major use of the Internet was to access external databases (Statistics Canada 1999).

Characteristics of the Internet

What is it about the Internet that is causing dramatic changes in learning and teaching? Is the Internet something we can do without in school, or will it become an essential resource? If we can't afford to ignore it, what are the features that make it important and what are the drawbacks to be avoided?

The Internet makes the same information available to everyone and is itself widely and easily accessible. It is a huge database of information with easy to use ways of searching for and finding what you want, and it makes the collected wisdom of experts in almost every specialist field available in the classroom. The Internet is global, dynamic and interactive, delivering text, colour, sound, graphics, film and full multimedia effects right into the classroom. Web pages are easily updatable – for example, news items appear online almost as the events happen. The Internet provides a means of communication with worldwide connectivity. The underlying complexity is belied by a surface simplicity; we send a message and it is immediately available to a named recipient anywhere in the world, or we publish a new web page and it is available to anyone, any-where. Every field of study can be explored in breadth and depth.

Accessibility

The Internet provides a delivery mechanism bringing resources directly into the school or home. There is a great deal of free educational material on the Internet so that it is seldom necessary to pay for information – an enormous benefit. Many websites provide material free of charge, which is always kept up to date. In addition, the same web pages can be available at school, at home, in libraries, in learning centres and in Internet 'cafés' so that homework projects started in class can be continued elsewhere. School web resources can be made available to pupils at home.

Reference and research

Now, as never before, we have easy access to up-to-date reference materials without having to make a visit to the library bookshelves. Indeed, few libraries can offer the range of reference material now available on the Internet and in the variety of forms suitable for different ages and purposes. Material not originally intended for education is also freely available for use in school. For example, by typing a street name or post-code into www.streetmap.co.uk you can immediately call up a map, with the scale clearly shown. You can see an aerial photo, zoom in to see a map showing individual buildings, or out to see a larger area, and you can move to neighbouring areas to the north, south, east or west (see Figure 6.1).

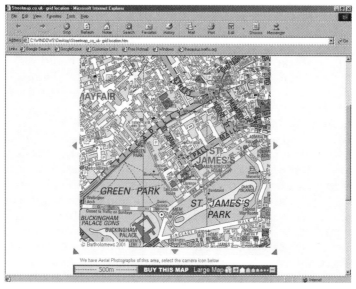

Figure 6.1 A street map accessed via the Internet

© Collins Bartholomew 2003

The ready accessibility of the Internet means that as questions come up in class the teacher can immediately find the answer and has available a powerful way of illustrating and explaining a concept. The Internet is also dynamic: using the map example, it is much more compelling to *see* the change in scale than simply to look at maps on paper. We can view film snippets, moving objects or sequences of images that have been programmed to explain ideas much more effectively than any 'still' picture or textual description ever could.

Interactivity

The Internet is interactive – as with the street map example, we are not limited to watching a prepared demonstration, we can also control and choose what we view so that different individuals can experiment, test and explore in ways that suit their own learning styles. Use of the Internet encourages and facilitates a spirit of enquiry and exploration. As an example, www.schoolsobservatory.org.uk/top.htm allows schools around the world to use world-class astronomical telescopes to make their own observations and the website provides a wealth of information for teachers and pupils. Projects are suggested for primary schools but the site is directed more to teachers and older students. In this case, as for many other subjects, the Internet provides for broad-ranging study but the user can follow links that go deeper and deeper into a subject.

'Fact Monster' (www.factmonster.com/mathmoney.html) is an award-winning site with material directly accessible to primary-age pupils and sections for subjects across the curriculum, including mathematics.

New learning and teaching skills

It is now possible for students to seek and find answers to their questions using the Internet, but they have to be taught how to do so. New teaching skills are therefore required to show children how to find reliable sources of information and how to interpret and understand web pages so that they can process the information and turn it into useful knowledge. The Internet can help to overcome the limitations of the available resources in the classroom and those of the teacher's own knowledge. Teachers need to feel comfortable with the fact that that they do not have to be all-round experts – when they don't know a subject well they can find out about it along with the children. Asking children to research the information and explain it to the teacher or to other children provides an excellent learning experience for them.

The interactive potential of the Internet means that it offers many opportunities for children to play mathematical games and solve problems, thereby gaining enjoyable practice in number work, exploring spatial relationships and developing their powers of reasoning and visualization.

However, we should question what advantage there is in having activities on the computer that could be done in the classroom with, for example, cards, counters or dice. There is no doubt that some computer-based games have little merit and the activities would be more effectively carried out with real objects. Teachers need to consider the advantages a particular computer-based version of an activity has to offer when compared to the more 'concrete' form of the activity. For example, the NRICH (pronounced 'enrich') website (www.nnch.maths.org) contains an adaptation of the well-known card game 'Pelmanism', where the objective is to find matching pairs (see Figure 6.2). The site also offers a suite of games to practise number bonds, multiplication tables, fractions, decimals and percentages. The games can be set at different levels of challenge, and there is a scoring system so that players are motivated to beat their best scores to date. One advantage is that the computer immediately checks everything the player does, so that the children learn from their own mistakes without intervention or judgement from anyone else. Because the computer sets up a new game so quickly, players can spend more time engaged in practising their skills within a given period of playing time.

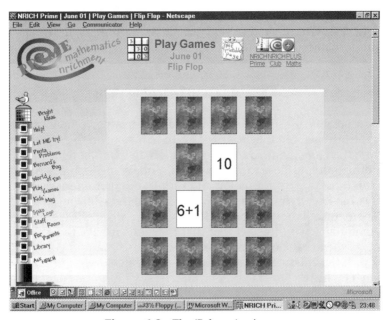

Figure 6.2   The 'Pelmanism' game

The Internet offers the opportunity of a 'global campus' style of learning. Students and teachers in different parts of the world communicate with each other, learn from each other, share ideas and work on tasks together using the Internet as a source of information and a means of communication. It also offers homework help services for students who want extra assistance.

Finally, a major potential drawback is for teachers to assume that the Internet can be simply added to their repertoire of classroom resources without considering the impact on the children's learning, and the implications for approaches to teaching. The Internet has characteristics not present in previous resources, and so teaching styles must be adjusted to take advantage of new learning opportunities.

Types of mathematics websites

There are, of course, many ways to classify websites related to mathematics education. One simple distinction can be made between those that supply free material and those that you must either pay to use or which advertise products for sale.

There are websites for fun and enrichment. Among the open access websites (free) there are those that are designed for children to use themselves for fun, where the material is often presented as written puzzles and problems or as interactive games (e.g. the online games at www.funbrain. com or at MathMagic at www.mathforum.org/mathmagic). Then there are websites designed to support schoolwork and homework, directed towards planned use in schools by teachers and likely to contain teaching-notes or lesson plans or have clearly identified mathematical learning objectives and perhaps links to a particular syllabus (e.g. the Birmingham school maths site – www.atschool.eduweb.co.uk/ufa10 – which, in addition to material for teachers, has compelling games on the pupils' page). To encourage children to take some responsibility for their own learning there are 'Homework help' and 'question/answer' services (e.g. askNRICH at www.nrich.maths.org/discus/messages/board-topics.html, or Ask Dr Math at www.mathforum.com/dr.math).

Other websites contain information for research on mathematical topics (e.g. on the history of mathematics at www-groups.dcs.st-andrews. ac.uk/~history/Indexes/HistoryTopics.html).

Choosing and evaluating a website

Browsing and casual 'surfing' for mathematics-related sites is fine if you have the time and just want to get an idea of what is 'out there'. However, your search is likely to be more productive if you have more purposeful motives. There are several key questions you should ask yourself before you begin searching the Internet. Once you have some idea of what you are looking for and why you want to find it, you have more chance of finding genuinely useful resources. It's a similar notion to the familiar saying, 'If you don't know where you are going, how will you know when you get there?' You need to ask yourself the following questions:

- Is the site I am looking for intended for use by children or by a teacher?
- What specific objectives or needs do I have in mind – concept development, skills practice, enrichment, specific topic research, demonstration model?
- What kind of use do I want – downloading, printing, on-screen interactive activities, information?
- If it's for use at school, what constraints are there likely to be – e.g. access to online computers, speed of connection?

Finding mathematics education websites

To get started you could use a general search engine (like Yahoo! or Google) and enter some key words like 'mathematics', 'education', children' or 'primary' ('math' and 'elementary' will help locate US sites). Increasingly, websites are now being 'meta-tagged', according to internationally agreed standards, to make it convenient to do advanced searches based on combinations of very specific criteria and to enable interoperability so that a search on one site will find relevant material on other similarly tagged sites. This system is a great improvement on earlier generations of search engines, yielding a smaller number of files relating to the desired content rather than bewilderingly long lists of not so well-matched items. However, to function well the system depends on the web content being expertly catalogued.

Another tactic is to use an Internet provider's home page, or a search engine provider's home page that lists categories such as news, travel and education, and begin by exploring their recommendations. Alternatively, you can begin with the website of a central organization such as a mathematics association, or in the UK the National Grid for Learning. These sites are likely to include links to recommended websites and may provide information about the nature of the content or links to the curriculum. Another way is to start with an address for a mathematics education website that you have been given, then look on that site for a 'links to other sites' section and use it as a gateway to similar sites.

Evaluating a website

The value of a website depends on what you expect to get out of it. Judgement about the suitability of a particular website is determined by

Table 6.2 Evaluating a website

Evaluation aspects	Questions for consideration
Structure and appearance	• Does it have an informative home page? • Does it have a clear section list or navigation bar? • Is it well laid out and easy to find your way around? • Does it have a search facility to help you find specific topics? • If it is for children's use – is it colourful and attractive? • Is it too cluttered or text dominated?
Content	• Does the material appear to be of good quality and is it all cost free? • Is the mathematical content at the right level, or organized in multiple levels? • Is there sufficient depth or choice of material? • Are the activities of the right type – e.g. problems, drill and practice, open-ended, games, interactive? • Is the material static or does it change regularly?
Usage potential	• Are there particular parts of the site suitable for individual, paired, small-group or whole-class use? • What level of teacher guidance would be required? • Is it suitable for independent use by children? • Are there good links for children to explore? • Do the activities need to be done at the computer, or can they involve students working away from the machine as well? • Is there communication potential, such as sending in solutions or emailing questions? • Does the site contain something useful for use as a teaching aid, for display or demonstration?
Practicalities	• Is download time for the site very slow? • Does it have feedback facilities or assessment/monitoring mechanisms for the teacher? • Can pages be easily printed or copied?

who the website is to be used by and what they want to do with it. Clearly, websites designed to give teachers lesson ideas won't be suitable for children, and sites with large amounts of text won't suit children with underdeveloped literacy skills. Similarly, websites designed for upper primary children won't suit very young children in mathematical content or language level, and so on. It is therefore somewhat impractical to devise a generic set of evaluation criteria because most aspects will be relative to the planned audience and type of use envisaged. However, it is still useful to focus on several factors when examining a website. Table 6.2 presents four aspects for consideration: structure and appearance, content, usage potential and practicalities.

Utilizing the Internet

Homework

The Internet can be used for homework if there are opportunities for all children to have access. Work introduced at school can be continued at home and with some school websites and intranets (i.e. local networks available only to a closed community of users) homework assignments can be set and submitted to the teacher electronically. Children may work from a CD that only requires them to be online when they use external links or when they are ready to submit their work. Teachers may give web addresses to parents or children to use informally at home or they may set homework assignments based on activites on the Internet or calling for children to do research for projects.

As time goes on more and more homes have Internet access and it is also available in many libraries and free learning centres open to the public. Numerous schools provide homework clubs and community learning centres so that all the children have the advantage of encouragement to learn and access to good resources. Equality of opportunity is very important, and families have a responsibility for their children's learning as well as the school. It has always been true that families who take their children to the library, have books at home and make learning an enjoyable part of life and family outings give their children enormous advantages. In today's world these experiences need to include technology and the Internet.

Games and activities

The Internet is a source of games and educational activities for motivation, particularly for practice and consolidation. Use of a computer suite for a whole class can be an advantage so that children can work individually or in pairs on games for mathematics practice, on other exercises taken from the Internet, on problem-solving online or on research for information for a project. Some primary teachers have found that splitting the class with half the pupils working on computers and half working with the teacher on parallel activities is motivating for the pupils, who enjoy both sorts of activity more because of the variety of learning involved.

Internet activities combined with other resources

Internet activities are best used to complement, or in combination with, other resources (e.g. books, worksheets, equipment and concrete materials, software, sharing sessions). Pupils can be rostered in pairs or small groups to use one or two available online computers or continue with other tasks until their turn comes. One system that often works well is that each pair has to explain to the next pair what they have to do. Other good learning experiences include investigating a topic on the Internet and than telling the class what they have learnt, or making a poster, a PowerPoint presentation or their own web pages.

There are opportunities via the Internet for the involvement of schools in contemporary scientific research that offer highly motivating experiences in learning science and data-handling opportunities for mathematics lessons. The Internet opens the classroom to the 'global campus' and allows children to be involved with the wider world of learning.

Open-ended tasks and differentiation

The Internet also provides a wealth of extension and enrichment activities for advanced students who need extra challenges leading on from activities that are suitable for all the children in the class, including children with learning difficulties.

One example is outlined here to show how a teacher can use one activity for a whole class but achieve differentiation through different learning objectives for different pupils according to their abilities, learning styles and needs. The investigation 'Teddy Town' (see www.nrich.maths.org/prime/may02/bbag.htm) is a simple combinatoric problem for children of all abilities and ages to solve in the 3 × 3 case (see Figure 6.3). Nevertheless this problem, in different contexts, has puzzled and engaged the world's best mathematicians, even though understanding its solutions requires only a knowledge of simple arithmetic. The objective is to arrange the houses and teddies on the grid so that no two houses of the same colour appear on the same line and no two teddies of the same colour appear on the same line. Practical equipment, such as coloured cups and saucers in a toy teaset, or coloured cards, can provide concrete experience alongside the computer activity.

So, why use the Internet for this activity and what are the learning objectives? In addition to the free supply of new ideas, the Internet provides more information for an advanced study of such problems. The learning objectives for all children could be the development of mathematical thinking and oral (possibly written) exposition. Additional learning objectives could be for pupils to develop symbolic recording of the arrangements; to develop systematic methods rather than trial and

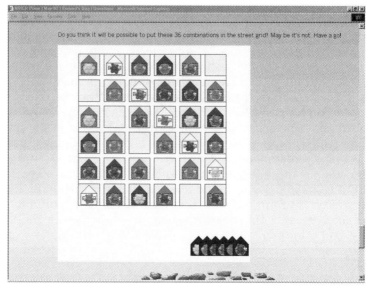

Figure 6.3 'Teddy Town'

error; to find a clear and concise way of giving instructions for solving the problem; to prove that there is no solution for the 2×2 case; to generalize their method from the 3×3 to the 4×4 and 5×5 cases; to classify the different solutions in each case; to establish that all solutions have been found; and finally to recognize that the methods do not generalize and that it is impossible to find a solution at all in the 6×6 case. As an extension activity, children could research the history of this type of problem on the Internet. Their search would rapidly lead them to the material on Latin Squares, and conjectures about the 6×6 case made in 1783 by Euler, one of the greatest mathematicians of all time. They will also discover that the 6×6 case was not fully explained by mathematicians until 1960. Instances such as this highlight the usefulness of the Internet in establishing links between the children's personal mathematical endeavours and the work of important mathematicians.

The best activities are open-ended so that children of all abilities, even those with learning difficulties, have success with the activity while at the same time there are challenges in the activity for the most able children in any class. The Teddy Town example is just one of many investigations provided by Bernard's Bag on the NRICH Prime website, suitable for 6–11-year-olds that are so open-ended that generalizations and proofs provide non-trivial challenges for the most able pupils and for older students.

Teaching ideas and preparation

When preparing lessons, teachers can locate ideas to enhance more traditional teaching – for example, interactive demonstrations or novel situations for problem-solving and mathematical thinking. They can find and print off material for children to use away from the computer. Many websites have a 'Get printable page' button that prints the content with high-resolution images but without the menu information from the web page or other 'clutter' that is not wanted on a printout. It is also easy to highlight, cut and paste material and to copy graphics from the Internet into Microsoft Word (or other word-processing programs) to make your own worksheets. It is necessary to check copyright conditions but many Internet sites allow copying for educational purposes as long as there is no commercial involvement. The Internet is also a good source for data collection and access to databases.

Teachers can do research to increase their own knowledge and understanding of particular topics. They can find and sample commercial products, such as mathematics software or online tutorials, and they can download pages and free software for use offline. They can also enter chat rooms and emailing discussion lists in order to share experiences and seek advice from other teachers and experts.

The Internet provides access to dynamic displays and interactive lesson material suitable for whole-class teaching where there is a large screen or data projector. There are many free sites and some by subscription (e.g. www.heymath.net). If the teacher has the use of an electronic whiteboard with its extra functionality, such resources can make whole-class teaching even more effective.

Extracurricular activity

The Internet provides resources for mathematics clubs or extracurricular activities. The NRICH Online Maths Club (see p. 104) was set up to offer sufficient resources so that busy teachers can run clubs without having to spend any time planning and preparing material.

Communication

Children's horizons are broadened through interaction with children, older students or teachers from other schools and other countries and through participation in online projects and live link-ups. Communication skills and self-confidence are boosted when children prepare work for publication on a class or school web page or to submit to the NRICH website (which publishes children's solutions to its puzzles and problems) or give live oral presentations via videoconferencing.

The NRICH Online Maths Club: an example of a mathematics community

Each mathematics education website has its own history, its own character, its own underlying philosophy and its own behind-the-scenes driving forces. The remainder of this chapter offers the reader the opportunity to understand the operation of a large and well-established website. While the site is unique, the case study allows the reader to consider the ways in which the dynamic features of the Internet may be utilized by both the creators and the users of any suitable website.

Overview of the NRICH Project

The NRICH Project provides curriculum enrichment and learning support for very able children of all ages, advice and in-service training for teachers, resources for mathematics clubs and peer assisted learning with help given by university students on an electronic answering service. NRICH engages students in problem-solving, publishes their work on the Internet and brings up-to-date materials to students and teachers in highly interactive ways. The purpose is to extend their awareness and understanding beyond the confines of the normal school programmes and heighten their appreciation of mathematics and its applications. Through services such as askNRICH and email talk groups, NRICH provides continuous and sustained support to help young people to maximize their potential and to make contact with other young people with similar talents and interests.

The main vehicle of the project is the set of three closely related websites catering for different age groups called NRICH Prime (5–12 years), NRICH Club ('main site', 11–19 years) and PLUS (17 years onwards). The underlying philosophy is that mathematics is a creative and exciting endeavour, and an individual's interest and talent in mathematics needs to be stimulated, stretched, challenged, articulated and shared. This way of thinking about mathematics education is reflected in the nature of the resources and services provided on the websites and by the project team 'in the field'.

Evaluations of the NRICH Project were carried out in 1997, 1998, 1999 and 2001. These studies provide some information about the ways in which the NRICH websites are being used and the impact they are having on teaching and learning.

Historical background

The NRICH Online Maths Club (www.nrich.maths.org.uk) is a free Internet service that provides a range of mathematics enrichment resources for teachers and students. (NRICH stands for National Royal Institution

Cambridge Homerton.) The main aim of the project is to support young, able mathematicians and their teachers and provide opportunities for mathematical enrichment beyond the limitations of set curricula. The NRICH website was set up by Toni Beardon and began with a pilot study in 1996 as a joint venture between the University of Cambridge School of Education, Homerton College, the Royal Institution of Great Britain and Norfolk Local Education Authority, funded by the University of Cambridge Local Examination Syndicate and the Royal Society through a Public Understanding of Science award.

The idea arose from an established Royal Institution project that supports a national network of special enrichment classes in mathematics held in different locations around the UK on Saturdays, often referred to as 'masterclasses'. These classes had been effective in stimulating and inspiring budding mathematicians for 15 years. An aspect of the master-class programme that is particularly valued by the participants is the social interaction with like-minded peers. Questions often asked at the end of a series of classes by the children and their parents are 'What do we do now? How can we find fun and challenging mathematics? We like to talk about mathematical things, can we keep in touch with our new friends from different schools?' The NRICH Project set out to address these questions in two ways. One was to provide a source of challenging material to support teachers in running 'maths clubs' or working with individuals. The second was to establish a communication network, using email and a web-board (chat room) for the children to use. Therefore, the notion of a 'club' is an important one for some users who, as regular visitors to the site, appreciate the sense of community and develop a rapport with other club members.

The project began by targeting 'middle school' years but has since expanded to cover the full range of secondary-level students, and with the launch of NRICH Prime, set up by Jenni Way in October 1998, it caters for children as young as 5 years. The NRICH Prime activities were funded for five years by the Clothworkers' Guild as part of a project involving the Royal Institution, the provision of interactive mathematics lectures for primary-school children in the historic lecture theatre at the Royal Institution and support for setting up primary masterclasses scattered around the UK. The amalgamation with NRICH of the PASS Maths website (located in the Cambridge University Department of Mathematics and Theoretical Physics and renamed PLUS) provided different types of articles for older students and adults. Although the project's prime purpose remains the support of young people with particular aptitude and interest in mathematics, the diverse age range covered means that there is material suitable for students at all stages of mathematical development. In 1999 the NRICH Project, along with several other compatible projects, joined a partnership with the Millennium Mathematics Project (www.mmp.org.uk) situated in Cambridge University's new Centre for Mathematical Sciences.

Usage statistics

The server for the NRICH website is equipped with software that automatically collects usage data, which is displayed to the public at www.nrich.maths.org/logs. It is difficult to interpret and draw confident conclusions from such statistics. For example, the increasing use of school and district intranets, particularly in the UK, means that that the NRICH site is being cached at many locations, which reduces the number of recorded hits to the site. Conversely, the rapid improvement of access to the Internet is likely to increase the number of accidental hits to the NRICH sites that result from browsing rather than serious use. Nevertheless, the statistics are useful for indicating general trends in use and allow the websites' personnel to monitor such things as the popularity of the sites as a whole in different countries, and the popularity of specific sections.

Data on the total number of hits to the NRICH sites is collected and the number has increased from an average of 4924 per day in October 1999 to 104,817 per day in March 2002. The increase in use is obviously assisted by the ever-increasing access to the Internet around the world.

At the end of March 2002 the three largest users of the websites, out of 112 countries, were the USA, the UK and Australia. Table 6.3 shows the

Table 6.3   Use of the NRICH websites in March 2002

	Hits		*User*
1	925380	28.48%	Unresolved/unknown
2	748289	23.03%	USA
3	594564	18.30%	UK
4	548706	16.89%	Network
5	118283	3.64%	Australia
6	37454	1.15%	Singapore
7	37335	1.15%	Canada
8	32519	1.00%	New Zealand
9	15026	0.46%	Japan
10	13785	0.42%	Non-profit organization
11	10943	0.34%	Spain
12	9635	0.30%	Denmark
13	9593	0.30%	France
14	7774	0.24%	Netherlands
15	7012	0.22%	South Africa
16	6825	0.21%	Belgium
17	6491	0.20%	Saudi Arabia
18	6265	0.19%	Hong Kong
19	5794	0.18%	Poland
20	5730	0.18%	Turkey

Source: www.nrich.maths.org/logs

top 20 users in terms of the number hits to the sites during March 2002. It should be noted that of 3.25 million hits that month, about 28 per cent were of unknown origin and a further 17 per cent were from within Cambridge University's internal computer network.

What is on the NRICH Prime website?

Websites are by nature flexible. Like many other websites, the NIRCH site is constantly being developed and improved. The description that follows presents a snapshot in time, so visitors to the site in the future might find some aspects have changed.

Collectively, the parts of the NRICH Prime website are meant to present mathematics as interesting, challenging and enjoyable for children aged 5 to 12 years. Mathematics is presented as something that takes place outside the classroom and around the world. Sometimes mathematical activity is entirely practical and useful, while at other times it is a purely abstract and fascinating way of thinking. The website promotes mathematical thinking as something to be shared, appreciated, respected and discussed.

Although anyone can access any of the sections on the website and use the material in any way they choose, various sections are prepared with distinct audiences in mind – children, teachers and parents. Table 6.4 indicates the intended audiences for each section. The material in most sections is changed on the first of each month and the previous month's material is archived in the library where it remains accessible to the public. Each month most of the material is on a particular mathematical theme or topic (e.g. fractions, coordinates) so that it provides a good collection of resources for teaching that topic.

Table 6.4 Finding your way around the NRICH Prime website

Type of material	Sections of website for each target audience		
	Teachers	Children	Parents
Problems, investigations and puzzles	Let Me Try Bernard's Bag Play Games World of Tan	Penta Problems Spike Logo Bernard's Bag Play Games World of Tan	Let Me Try World of Tan
Information and inspiration	Staffroom Bright Ideas	Kids' Mag	For Parents
Communication with peers	Primath email list AskNRICH Web Board	NRICHTalk	

Website production steps

The primary editor writes material, collects material from contributing authors and puts together the sections. Solutions to problems sent in by children are processed and prepared for publication. The prepared material, mostly in electronic form, is given to the webmaster. Computer officers and assistants build the 'new' website alongside the current 'live' site. Illustrations and diagrams are added to the text. On-screen interactive items are designed. Much of the material is classified and tagged into the searchable database. The 'new' site is checked and edited before 'going live'. On the first of the month the 'new' site replaces the old to become the 'current month', and most components of the 'old current month' are stored in the relevant parts of the library section.

NRICH Prime website content

Two sections, Penta Problems and Kids' Mag are intended for direct access by children of about 8 to 12 years of age and are written in a style and language level suitable for that age group so that the ideas and mathematics are accessible with little or no intervention from adults. (Despite the deliberate focus on the children themselves, Penta Problems is actually the most popular part of the website with teachers.)

The Penta Problems section consists of a set of five 'closed' problems, with a new set published each month, all usually on the same topic and hence providing a useful collection for teachers when they come to teach that topic. Although there are often multiple answers and many paths to an answer, the nature of the problems are such that the children usually know themselves when they have solved the problem. Children are encouraged to send in solutions by email, fax or mail (one boy from Singapore likes to send PowerPoint presentations of his work). Some come from schools via a teacher, but many come from home. Full solutions and explanations of thinking and strategies are expected rather than simple answers. The editor processes the responses sent in and selects a range of solutions for publication on the website the following month. Efforts are made to acknowledge as many individuals and schools as possible. The children's work is the only form of solution presented on the website. There are some regular contributors, both school groups and individuals. Although the age of the contributors ranges from 6 to 12 years, most solutions come from 9- and 10-year-olds. The majority come from England, but there are usually some answers from Australia and Singapore and at least two other countries such as Scotland, the USA, Turkey, Israel, New Zealand or Canada. This not only provides motivation for students to produce good quality responses, but also provides them with insight into the way other people think about the problems, as indicated in the following comments from users:

I printed off the one where our children's solution was shown on the web page, which was a great thrill for our kids. I have also printed off one or two others which have fascinated them, to see how other groups of children approach and solve them.

(Primary teacher, NRICH evaluation 1998)

I look at how different users have different methods to reach a solution. Look for my name and see if I've been mentioned. If I got one wrong or I found one a problem, so I didn't send off my solution, I'd look at the answer, so I can learn something from it.

(Pupil, NRICH evaluation 1998)

The children enjoy finding the problems on the Internet and it gives their work an extra boost if they think they can send in their answers.

(Primary teacher, NRICH evaluation 1999)

Below is an example of a Penta Problem published on the website in June 2000, followed by the set of solutions that were published the following month. Note how the editor has tried to highlight a range of approaches used by the children.

On the planet Vuv there are two sorts of creature. The Zios have three legs and the Zepts have seven legs.

The great planetary explorer Nico, who first discovered the planet, saw a crowd of Zios and Zepts. He managed to see that there was more than one of each kind of creature before they saw him. Suddenly they all rolled over onto their backs and put their legs in the air.

He counted 52 legs. How many Zios and how many Zepts were there?

Well, everyone agreed that there must be eight Zios and four Zepts, but not everyone worked it out the same way! Daniel (age 10, from an Anglo-Chinese primary school in Singapore) drew a table (see Figure 6.4), whereas these 8-year-olds from Wesley College Prahan prep school in Melbourne Australia took a different approach:

Kev: I got that answer by $7 \times 4 + 3 \times 8 = 52$, the total number of legs he saw.
Dougall: I started counting backwards from 52 and I counted the Zios first and then I counted the Zepts second.
Nick: I drew circles with three legs and circles with seven legs.

Mark and Stuart (age 9, from Cummersdale Lower Junior School in the UK) used calculation and tables facts to solve the problem:

I wrote down both times tables and added the numbers together and got, four Zepts and eight Zios; and two Zios and two Zepts times two is 40, add four Zios is 52, four Zepts and eight Zios.

Zios(3)	Zepts(7)	Legs	✗ or ✓
2	2	20	✗
3	3	30	✗
10	3	51	✗
8	4	52	✓

Figure 6.4   Daniel's solution table

This method, using multiplication tables, was explained in detail by Clementine and Laura (age 11, from the Mount School, York, UK), who began by listing multiples of Zios (three) and then checking the number of Zepts (seven) needed to make the total of 52 legs.

Charlotte, Sarah and Kate (age 11, from The Mount School) and Christina (age 10, from Malborough Primary, UK) started the other way around – first the multiples of Zepts (seven), then the Zios (three).

Emma and Eleanor (age 11, from The Mount School) and Elizabeth (age 12, from Stamford High School, Lincolnshire, UK), realized that the number of Zio legs (three) plus the number of Zept legs (seven) make ten legs. Hence they worked with pairs of Zios and Zepts – i.e. multiples of ten:

$3 + 7 = 10$
$10 \times 4 = 40$ and $52 - 40 = 12$, which is 3×4
So there are 4 Zepts and 8 Zios

Lucy and Sarah (age 12, from Stamford High School) each found a way of starting with the total number of legs (52), then taking it apart into numbers that were multiples of 3 or 7. They thought about division, rather than multiplication. Sarah said:

I found this by taking away 3 and then dividing by 7 and if it divides into a whole number that was the answer. If it did not divide into a whole number I took away 6 and so on until I found the answer. Then I took the number of legs of the Zepts away from 52 and divided it to find the number of Zios.

Lucy said:

You have to find two numbers which add up to 52 and one has to divide by three and the other by seven:

$28 + 24 = 52$
$28 \div 7 = 4$
$24 \div 3 = 8$

The Kids' Mag is a magazine style section for children and is intended to help them to see mathematics from fresh perspectives that are not usually made apparent in school classrooms. It reveals mathematics as a social and cultural activity, as having origins in both the distant past and more recent history, as being creative, artistic and even humorous. Sometimes it becomes the vehicle for cultural appreciation when the entire Kids' Mag encompasses aspects of a particular country's mathematics, education and art, usually inspired by the primary editor's contact with that country through collaborative projects or education conferences. For example, the July and September 2000 editions focused on India and included items on old Indian measuring devices, an Indian mythology website, an ancient game and how to draw traditional symmetrical Rangoli designs. The themes sometimes spill over into Penta Problems and even into the teachers' magazine, Staffroom.

Kids' Mag has several regular items, beginning with Chit Chat, which is intended to personalize the web page and give a 'club' or 'community' feeling. This section is often used to send greetings to children and schools that the primary editor has had contact with during the previous month, as well encouragement to send in solutions, try new activities or appreciate a particular content theme.

Funny Maths contains mathematical jokes or a 'Dry Rot' cartoon (see Figure 6.5) contributed by a mathematics educator from Australia. It features children and a teacher struggling with each other's mis-understandings and strange interpretations of mathematical ideas or terminology.

Mouldy Maths and Look! are usually tied together by a common theme.

Figure 6.5 The 'Dry Rot' cartoon

Mouldy Maths looks back in time to reveal people, discoveries and events that have built the mathematics of today's world. The text is kept fairly brief and is accompanied by pictures and diagrams. 'Hotlinks' to other websites or articles within the NRICH site are located within the text to provide more detailed information, including mathematical details. The Look! section alerts children to other websites, books and resources, usually related to the topic covered in Mouldy Maths. The purpose is to stimulate new mathematics-related interests in children, as well as to provide the opportunity for further research. For example, the May 2001 Kids' Mag theme was polygons and stars. Mouldy Maths talked about the mapping of the stars long ago using astrolabes and provided hotlinks to further historical information as well as modern astronomy websites.

Making Maths is for those children who enjoy exploring mathematical ideas through manipulating materials. This section is about investigating mathematics through art, craft, designing and making. Enthusiasts use the activities as springboards for hours of investigations and produce creative visual displays of their discoveries.

The rest of the NRICH website, although aimed as secondary school students, also contains a lot of material suitable for the older primary pupils, particularly the games and problems in the Monthly Six. Many of these problems do not require any more mathematics than children would have met by the age of 10 or 11. One example is the problem called Nine Colours, from the April Six in 2001 (see Figure 6.6), where the children can click and drag the small coloured cubes into position.

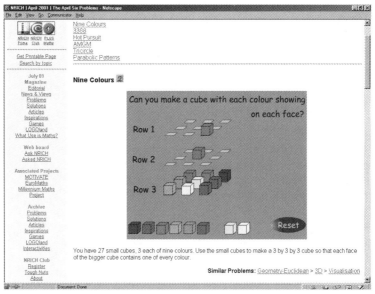

Figure 6.6   Nine Colours is a good example of interactive online problem-solving

The mathematical activities in the Bernard's Bag section are open-ended investigations, which means they provide starting points for the exploration and discovery of a range of mathematical patterns and relationships. Although some guidance is provided through the presentation of the investigations in a series of steps, children are encouraged to make their own decisions about directions for further exploration. They are encouraged to pose their own questions and change the parameters of the original investigation, particularly when considering the question 'I wonder what would happen if . . .?'

The open-ended nature of these mathematical tasks means that there is no limit placed on the degree of sophistication of mathematical thinking that can be applied. Chosen pathways of investigation can be terminated with satisfaction at a basic solution level or pursued until generalizations can be made and proofs developed.

Bernard's Bag is supported by teachers' notes that are designed to assist teachers who may not be familiar with this type of mathematical activity or the mathematics that may emerge during the investigation. Although there is evidence indicating that this section is well used, children and teachers rarely send in work for publication.

The Let Me Try section contains two problems or investigation designed for 5- to 8-year-olds, to be tackled with the support of an adult. Teachers' notes are provided to assist in the presentation and development of the task, particularly when used with a group or class of children.

The Play Games section is intended to be easily accessible to teachers, children and parents. Instructions are simple and the equipment needed is minimal – things like counters and matchsticks. Some games include an interactive version, but in general they are designed to be played away from the computer, usually in pairs, so that a whole class can participate. The games are easy to start playing, but all provide plenty of opportunity for mathematical thinking when trying to develop winning strategies. Suggestions for adapting and investigating the mathematics behind the games are given. For example, the game of Two Stones (published on the February 1999 site) only requires four counters and a simple game board that can be easily drawn (see Figure 6.7). Anyone can start sliding the counters around, but just how do you trap your opponent? How do you prevent yourself being trapped? Only a careful study of move sequences will reveal the secret! Try it!

The Staffroom magazine is for teachers and other adults. The Resource Review section covers a variety of websites, published books and other teaching materials. The other major feature is the monthly article, which presents research and theory behind teaching ideas as well as practical activities. Some articles link to in-service courses and workshops run by NRICH, and so provide support material for participants.

The World of Tan section is for everyone, though the story is written at a language level suitable for about 8 years upward. Each month there is a

In China this game is known as *Pong hau k'i* and in Korea it is called *Ou-moul-ko-no*. It looks easy but actually takes some thought and good strategies. The game is for two players. You will need a game board, which is very easy to draw, and each player needs two counters or buttons (the stones).

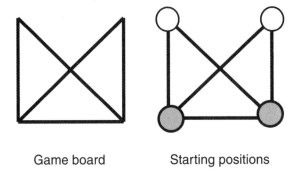

Game board   Starting positions

Place two stones at the top and two at the bottom as shown.
(At the start of the next game the players should swap positions.)
The players take turns at sliding one stone along a line to an empty spot (so the first move will always be to the middle). To win, you have to block the other player so he or she can't move.

Figure 6.7   The game of Two Stones

short episode on the lives of Grandma Tan and her Chinese family, followed by suggested activities for children, teachers and parents. A key feature is one or more silhouettes that can be made by fitting together the seven traditional tangram shapes.

The Spike Logo section is based on a version of Logo software, specifically designed for young children, that can be downloaded from the NRICH website. Spike, a rather adorable little spider, provides a series of tutorials and challenges for children.

The Bright Ideas section contains a bank of ideas for special mathematical activities such as maths fun days, field trips or competitions. It is gradually added to rather than changed every month. Teachers are encouraged to contribute, and some ideas are collected from the teachers' email talk list.

With a large number of children accessing the site from home, it was decided to offer some specific support to parents, particularly those of bright, enthusiastic young mathematicians. The For Parents section offers advice on how to make best use of the various sections of the website, as well as referring people to other relevant organizations and websites. Thirty-one parents completed the NRICH 1999 evaluation – here are some of their comments:

> I look for interesting math problems for my 8-year-old son. Not that he is a genius, but the usual additions and subtractions which he gets as homework bore him.
> (Parent from Oman, NRICH evaluation 1999)

> Me and my 10-year-old son have a monthly contest as to who can answer the most questions correctly!
> (Parent from England, NRICH evaluation 1999)

> It is suitable for gifted children. My daughter attends school and is significantly under-challenged, so she benefits by using NRICH at home.
> (Parent from England, NRICH evaluation 1999)

Mathematical interaction and communication

The emphasis on the communication between and among the NRICH personnel and the website users is a characteristic that distinguishes this website from many others. As already mentioned, children are encouraged to send in solutions for publication on the website the following month. Further interaction takes place through the use of email and web-board discussions about problems, mathematical topics, issues and resources. Several thousand primary teachers and other interested adults subscribe to the NRICH Primath email list, and students have access to the NRICHtalk email list. All emails are moderated by NRICH staff to ensure appropriate content.

Many students (mainly secondary) also make use of the askNRICH web board to hold discussions about mathematic-related topics. This web board contains a free members only section supported by over 50 university mathematics students, where children can ask questions about mathematics that is new to them. This interaction using technology has relieved the feeling of isolation that many very able students experience, and given them access to mathematical people and ideas:

> It's brilliant. I can ask all the questions I want. The answers are fascinating because they take you further than you were asking plus you can have a decent conversation with someone who knows much more maths than you.
> (Student aged 17, NRICH evaluation 1998)

Although the askNRICH service is used less frequently by primary-aged children, occasionally a very bright young mathematician benefits greatly from the opportunity to explore ideas well beyond the set school curriculum. The exchange recorded below took place at the end of 1998, when Lucy, aged 9, posted a message on the NRICH web board. The conversation is with Dave, one of the team of university students who did his best to keep in mind Lucy's age. He was amazed at the outcome!

Lucy's question
Hello, I am Lucy. My maths teacher gave me a number of questions from Cambridge Primary Mathematics [a textbook series]. Let me give you one:

A pencil, rubber and notebook cost £1.
The notebook costs more than two pencils.
Three pencils cost more than two rubbers.
Three rubbers cost more than a notebook.
What is the least possible cost of the pencil? 15p
What is the greatest possible cost of a pencil? 26p

OK so I've got the answer but it was a bit tedious trying this and that. If it was equals instead of more than I could have changed it into equations and cancelled down I guess, but I'm sure there is a better way, or do they just want to waste my time?
Thanks
Lucy

Dave's response
Hi Lucy! Yes of course there is . . . If there's a will there's a way! I am *not* going to give you the complete solution, *but* I will give you the following hints. If you want the greatest cost, then you want your two pencils to cost as much as the notebook; similarly, if you want your pencil to cost the least, then you want your three pencils to cost at least as much as two rubbers.

Now you might want to consider fractions, like if three pencils cost as much as two rubbers, then a rubber costs as much as 3/2 pencils. Also, keep an eye out that the total cost is £1 and then the other two conditions, after you get rid of one unknown item by using fractions as described above, will give you bounds like (HINT) '9/2 pencils cost more than a notebook but cost less than two pencils'.

So the above condition gives you feasible solutions. Pick the number of pencils to replace the notebooks to give you the maximum or minimum. See what simplifications you can make, and tell me how you get on.

PS: the exact answer is 300/11 = 27.27 (two decimal places) for the greatest cost and 100/7 = 14.29 (two decimal places) for the least cost. So you are correct, if corrected to the nearest pence. Anyway, tell me how you get on.
Yours
Dave

Lucy's reply
Dear Dave, thanks very much for the tips. I think I managed to solve it. Here goes:

p (p = pencil n = notebook r = rubber) + r + n = 100
the n costs more than 2p
3p costs more than 2r
3r costs more than a n

For the highest value of p
n = 2p
3r = n
p + r + n = 100
p + r + 2p = 100
3r = n = 2p
r = 2/3p
p + 2/3p + 2p + 100
11p/3 = 100
p = 27.27

For least value of p
3p = 2r
3r = n
p + 3/2 + n = 100
p + 3/2p + 9/2p = 100
14p/2 = 7p = 100
p = 14.29

Thanks it was really fun. I enjoyed it! If you could give me another one of the same type it would be really good. We are doing fractions at school but I have to learn the basics (yawn) and I don't get many really fun problems.
From
Lucy

Dave's response
Lucy,
I have to say I was totally blown away by your solution. I didn't really expect you to do it and I'm sure that I couldn't do that when I was your age! Anyway, this type of problem (i.e. maximize the cost of pencils under given conditions or constraints) is called an Optimization problem. The one you did is in the class of problem called linear programming problems.

Dave then went on to give Lucy some real-life examples of this kind of problem which showed the need to test the validity of a solution in a particular context. Then he set her a similar kind of problem about shoes that included probability. Lucy solved this and begged for more!

Using material from the website

Information from the evaluation surveys, together with informal observations and inquiries by NRICH staff have revealed that NRICH is being used in a variety of ways. The problems and investigations are being incorporated by teachers into their mathematics lessons and as additional enrichment beyond the curriculum, particularly for more able or enthusiastic children. Penta Problems and Bernard's Bag register as the most frequently visited sections.

Many teachers (58 per cent of primary and secondary teachers in the 1999 evaluation) encourage their pupils to access the site themselves and some draw on NRICH to support maths clubs run outside of normal class time:

> I use it as a resource for class problem-solving and investigation lessons, changing the problems as needed to suit the children. The children enjoy the problems, and are enthusiastic about maths as a result.
>
> (Primary teacher in English rural school,
> NRICH evaluation 1999)

> I use the problems with more able children who are withdrawn from the classroom all across the junior age range, but I also use them with a maths club I run that is open to every pupil.
>
> (Primary teacher in English suburban school,
> NRICH evaluation 1999)

> I download the problem pages once a month to put on the school intranet. I make the pupils aware of its presence but I have no way of monitoring how frequently it is used. I also print out problems from time to time for class use.
>
> (Teacher from English private preparatory school,
> NRICH evaluation 1999)

NRICH material is used by teachers in class lessons, for homework and in special maths clubs. However, an important fact revealed by the 1998 evaluation was that 26 per cent of the children responding to the online survey used the NRICH material at home without the support of their teacher or interaction with classmates. The 1999 evaluation suggested this figure was even higher.

Changes in teaching and learning

Information from the 1998 evaluation provided indications of improved problem-solving skills as well as changes in teaching and learning styles and attitudes. This was reported by 91 per cent of teachers who said that the students' problem-solving skills had improved as a result of using NRICH material. Also, 57 per cent of teachers reported changes in their teaching style. Comments about improved communication of mathematics and more positive perceptions of the subject were often offered:

> They are becoming more confident in knowing the steps to take to solve a problem and are more willing to try out different approaches.
> (Primary teacher, NRICH evaluation 1998)

> Most problems have encouraged children to look at any problem in a number of ways and communicate with other people in order to solve the problem more quickly and efficiently.
> (Primary teacher, NRICH evaluation 1998)

> It can be fun! Many different aspect of maths. Learnt more about logic. Enjoyable and challenging maths.
> (Student aged 12 years, NRICH evaluation 1998)

Although the positive influence of NRICH was not as obvious in the 1999 evaluation data, there was still some evidence of the influence of participation in the NRICH services, with 46.8 per cent of the surveyed pupils saying that NRICH had made them more interested in mathematics. This is supported by 49.1 per cent of the teachers (both primary and secondary) saying that using NRICH had made their pupils more interested in mathematics:

> All the problems are challenging to me, not like the problems I do at school. Doing the problems has made me feel how it feels to be stuck on a mathematics problem and not know how to do it.
> (Pupil aged 11 years from Singapore,
> NRICH evaluation 1999)

> I think NRICH is really cool and has made me think differently about mathematics.
> (Pupil aged 12 years from the USA,
> NRICH evaluation 1999)

Teachers also reported changes in their own attitudes and practice:

> Very grateful for the service. I feel less isolated now that I have discovered the site and have been encouraged to let the children innovate and experiment more.
> (Primary teacher, NRICH Evaluation 1998)

> NRICH has increased my personal interest and enjoyment of maths as a teacher (and maths coordinator). I am about to start a maths club based on NRICH.
> (Primary teacher, from English inner-city school,
> NRICH evaluation 1999)

In the research study focusing on school-age children conducted in May/June 2001, with questionnaires to be filled in and submitted on the NRICH website, the NRICH team pursued the question 'What is the impact of the Internet on learning mathematics?' Children compared their experience of learning mathematics with the Internet to other ways of learning. In this study there was a range of responses and not all were as positive about the use of computers, or about mathematics, as those quoted below:

> Because I'm home-schooled I find doing things on the computer more fun. And I can do the games, where I'm learning at the same time as enjoying myself! Just doing it on paper isn't as good, and you can't do the games!
>
> (Student aged 14 years from the UK,
> NRICH Evaluation 2001)

> I'm really bad at maths but am trying to get better, and it's these kinds of sites that have made me more interested in it. Maths was boring, but now maybe it's starting to be fun.
>
> (Student aged 14 years from the UK,
> NRICH evaluation 2001)

> I am top of my class at maths and most of the topics that we cover are just revision for me. I very much enjoy solving the problems on NRICH as it makes me think a lot more.
>
> (Student aged 11 years from the UK,
> NRICH evaluation 2001)

> School does not encourage academic competition. Nor does it promote learning for the sake of learning and discovering new things. Education, at school, is something that is simply memorized, then applied over and over. You can get through without thinking quite easily.
>
> (Student aged 18 years from Australia,
> NRICH evaluation 2001)

The Internet supports groups who share similar interests, enabling them to communicate with each other and the NRICH Online Maths Club is one such community. This is what one of the members had to say in relation to the statement 'NRICH makes me feel I belong to a club or community':

> I agree because normally not many people are interested in maths and you often try to find somebody with as much interest. This task is normally quite hard but when you log onto NRICH you feel like you are among friends.
>
> (Student aged 11 years from the UK,
> NRICH evaluation 2001)

Conclusion

Although NRICH is one of the oldest websites of its type and is now very well established, there is still a general feeling that it has only just begun to make use of the enormous potential for learning that the Internet offers. The impact of the Internet on both the learning and teaching of mathematics is the subject of ongoing research. However, websites such as NRICH have already achieved at least one thing: in the words of a secondary teacher, 'It has helped spread the idea that maths can be something the world can do together'.

References

Australian Bureau of Statistics (2000) *Media release, November 2000: Australian Children Log On.* wwww.abs.gov.au (accessed January 2003).

Computer Economics (1999) *Media Usage: Computers and the Internet.* www.media-awareness.ca/issues/usenet.htm (accessed December 2002).

National School Boards Foundation (2000) *The Programs: Safe & Smart.* www.nsbf.org/safe-smart/index.html (accessed December 2002).

NOP Research Group (2000) *Survey Results: Net Use Soars Among UK Kids.* www.nop.co.uk (accessed January 2002).

Statistics Canada (1999) *The Daily: news releases: previous issues: 15 July.* www.statcan.ca (accessed December 2002).

7

CLASSROOM TECHNOLOGIES AS TOOLS NOT TOYS: A TEACHER'S PERSPECTIVE ON MAKING IT WORK IN THE CLASSROOM

Merilyn Buchanan

Introduction

This chapter is one primary school mathematics teacher's account of her own learning journey into what was for her uncharted territory. There is always fear and resistance about stepping from a comfortable, familiar place into unknown realms. My inspiration and challenge to take the first steps into the realm of technology came from encounters with three influential people. My journey was in three phases: the first was facing up to the need for change, the second was the planning phase and the third was implementing and evaluating the changes brought about by embedding technology into the mathematics curriculum.

Influences and inspiration

'I began to see the light'; 'It was a turning point'; 'A true revelation'. These three rather dramatic phrases sound as though some spiritual transformation took place. In fact they describe the impact of three influential people who helped me reflect upon, and ultimately change, my rather catholic practice.

I thought I had heard *all* of the arguments about why teachers should change their practice to incorporate technology across the curriculum. However compelling the rationales seemed, I was very resistant and worked extremely hard to stave off change and maintain my personal status quo. So, for me to embrace and implement change would require a dramatic transformation. However, the transforming experiences did not come dramatically but in a rather mundane way: they were professional development days.

Well, in fairness, they weren't mundane. The key speaker at the first event was David Thornberg, billed as a 'futurist'. Hmmm, futurist, that didn't sound as though it was going to inspire me to infuse more technology into my teaching as promised. The promise had come from the school technology coordinator, the second influential person, who worked tirelessly to meet the needs of the staff. She took the position of pushing gently from behind and coming forward enthusiastically when teachers expressed a need to use technology to enhance a programme or enrich learning opportunities. As part of her master plan she organized speakers in the hope of at least piquing interest if not inspiring. Interesting, inspirational speakers were arranged for our teacher development days and local schools, and any interested student teachers, were invited to participate.

The modern digital computer, invented a little over 50 years ago, has multiplied in power and availability to the point where over half of the homes in the USA have computers that exceed the power of the mainframe computers of the 1970s. Annual sales of computers now exceed the sales of television sets. Gordon Moore, the chief scientist at Intel, has claimed that the power of microchip technology doubles every 18 months. The information explosion we are experiencing has no apparent end. A child born today is exposed to more information in one year than his grandparents were exposed to in their entire lifetimes (ignoring the probability that the grandparents are still alive!) Think of the implication of all of that for the growth of access to information. But, I asked myself, what does it imply for the teaching of mathematics, a domain that is regarded as having a fairly circumscribed body of knowledge?

'We [continue to] prepare students for our past not their future, despite the fact the future is changing because it is being created every day' (Thornberg 1996). That statement, or perhaps indictment from Thornberg, resonated with me and would become my nemesis. It connected with what I knew of Lortie's (1975) seminal work on teachers' practices, which he characterized as internalized *conservatism* and *presentism*. How teachers carry out their work stems from a long 'apprenticeship of observation' which ensures that practice is 'wedded to the past' and that we teach as we were taught. The natural order of the classroom, it seems, is to prepare pupils for their futures by using methods from our pasts. In total, our pupils are well prepared with outmoded knowledge and skills to function effectively in obsolete systems.

There is a huge difference between knowledge on the one hand and understanding or insight on the other, as the third of the trio of influential people, Jamie McKenzie pointed out on yet another professional development day: 'While knowledge is important it cannot be the ultimate goal of learning activities'. If this statement is accepted then didactic method, *teaching as telling*, has to be called to account. It becomes foolish to assume that teachers can fill students' minds by 'teaching' them information that will last them a lifetime.

School mathematics programmes often centre on engaging students in accumulating information or collecting answers. McKenzie argued that curricula should be driven by essential questions. Essential questions are central to our lives. They require students to spend time pondering the meaning, importance and validity of information. They call for our best thinking and touch upon issues that define what it means to be human. They are questions that help us to make meaning out of the cumulative events and circumstances of our lives. As central, meaningful and important as mathematical understandings and enquiries are, could I find a way of using essential questions to drive mathematical learning experiences in a primary classroom?

In total, the comments and ideas that Thornberg and McKenzie put forward have profound implications for the classroom. It is time to challenge the traditions of our educational systems and to re-evaluate the needs of people who need to be able to function effectively in the new global society. The division between teaching and learning blurs as we, the whole classroom community, are required to keep on learning together as we move into our futures. After all, who could possibly master the ever-expanding body of knowledge?

The quest becomes one of finding ways throughout the curriculum to manage most effectively the vast quantities of easily accessed information. Yet, for all of its present impact and dilemmas, it seems that this information age and what we know will remain less important than what we can invent, and the capacity for invention comes from the understandings that we construct for ourselves. Piaget's (1973) notion of *constuctivism* rather than *instructivism* is a concept that has come of age. We have to move beyond the information age and prepare students for the *creativity age* of their future.

With these ideas in mind, the technology coordinator held a staff meeting. Teachers brainstormed, agreed and committed to a school-wide philosophy that stated:

- It is no longer feasible to impart abundant information to students and expect them to remember and use it in meaningful ways.
- It is no longer feasible to have students work in isolation, unaware of their global surroundings.

- No longer can we limit students to working on simple solutions to simple problems.
- Common to all learning is the belief that students must make sense of their world; that they must solve complex problems requiring critical thinking skills; that they must be able to communicate and collaborate; and we, the adults, must provide them with the tools to accomplish these tasks.

I agreed to these ideals in principle – the time to face the future was now – but I was left with a practical question: how could all of this be enacted in mathematics?

Reflection

The mathematics programme I presented seemed to be successful: children declared that they enjoyed mathematics lessons, that they found them interesting, that they felt as though they were learning. Exam results were high and the programme did not feel sterile or driven by exam content. Parents seemed satisfied and the principal didn't complain. There was no pressure, no *reason* to change. I was a fully paid up member of the 'If the class isn't broken, why fix it!' way of thinking that Jamie McKenzie had referred to. I knew about the available technologies, I could use them if I needed to; I simply didn't *need* to change.

Change, that is, from using technology here and there as a supplement to learning, making worksheets look more attractive, more motivational, with a touch of clipart here and having children stamp pictures there because they think it's fun and I could argue (at a stretch) that it met information and communication technology (ICT) requirements. A change in practice would mean not installing 'drill and kill' software packages in an attempt to ensure that basic facts were firmly installed in pupils' long-term memories. It would mean a change from regarding 'technology' as something bolted onto the planned learning experiences, a token of modernism. If I was to attend to all of the buzz phrases and consider 'meaningfully incorporating a variety of technologies' as 'central, supporting tools of learning' then change of that proportion would mean reflection on purpose, on exploring how, why, when and where technology could make a substantive difference.

No wonder resistance is so attractive. Change is easy when you simply advise others to engage in it and don't have to plan and implement it. Nonetheless, I was spurred on by the fact that I was beginning to acknowledge a need for *some* change on behalf of the children I was responsible for and I was motivated by the belief that I was moving positively into the new millennium. Perhaps I'd change one of the units that I taught. It would be an experiment, action research, a personal challenge, an enquiry into change. The change would be from 'I' as the subject to 'they' and from 'my past' to 'their future'.

If I was to accept the challenge, it would be to plan and manage opportunities for pupils aged 11 to 13 to engage in meaningful and substantive mathematics-based enquiry that would take full advantage of the technologies that we had available in the school. I would have to find a way to ensure that the unit would have structure, yet would be responsive to pupils' emerging interests. The challenge would require that as the pupils investigated, researched, collected and collated information and communicated their findings, they would find the need for (and a reason to) learn how to use specific technologies and acquire new skills.

Purpose and principles

I wasn't going to change for change's sake. I tried to be reflective and thoughtful about the reason for changing my practice and the goals I was hoping to achieve. To help me articulate these I looked at the *Principles and Standards 2000 for School Mathematics* published by the National Council of Teachers of Mathematics (NCTM 2000) as well as the draft of the *Mathematics Framework for California Public Schools (K-12)* (California State Department of Education 2000). The *Framework* has been greatly impacted by recommendations from the NCTM and there is considerable correspondence between the content or process standards and the objectives for the same age groups in the National Numeracy Strategy (NNS) (DfEE 1999).

There was one goal in particular I kept in mind from the *Framework* which related to offering a challenging learning experience that would help maximize achievement and provide meaningful opportunities for all learners. I also wanted to ensure that the concept of 'essential questions' (as described by McKenzie) determined the enquiry. Most importantly, the focus must be on learning mathematics, using technology as a tool, rather than the technology becoming an end in itself.

The goals for pupils were several. The study should assist learners in:

- Developing understanding of mathematical concepts and fluency in basic skills as well as the ability to use reasoning to solve mathematical problems.
- Communicating precisely about quantities and relationships through the use of signs, symbols, models, graphs and mathematical terms.
- Gathering and analysing evidence and building arguments to support or disprove hypotheses.
- Making connections among mathematical ideas as well as between mathematics and other disciplines.
- Applying mathematics to everyday life situations and developing and sustaining an interest in mathematics.

- Appreciating the power and fascination of mathematics and how it enriches their lives.

What materials, equipment and technological support would facilitate reaching such ideological goals? *Principles and Standards 2000 for School Mathematics* (NCTM 2000) recommends that:

- Every student should have access to an appropriate calculator.
- Every mathematics teacher should have access to a computer with appropriate software and network connections for instructional and non-instructional tasks.
- Every mathematics classroom should have computers with Internet connections available at all times for demonstrations and students' use.
- Every school mathematics programme should provide students and teachers with access to computers and other appropriate technology for individual, small-group, and whole-class use, as needed, on a daily basis.

I could meet these recommendations for equipment and add to the list, but what would be added to the mathematics programme? *Principles and Standards 2000* states that 'Technology should not be used as a replacement for basic understandings and intuitions; rather, it can and should be used to foster those understandings and intuitions. In mathematics instruction programs, technology should be used widely and responsibly, with the goal of enriching students' learning of mathematics' (NCTM 2000). I liked the sentiment but still wondered how 'wide and responsible use' would and could enrich the experience for all children.

Personal principles of practice

It is important to mention my own beliefs and preferred teaching style, as these idiosyncratic factors were crucial as I planned and implemented the unit of study.

- I believe that mathematics learning is more effective and enduring if units of study are designed to emphasize the rich interconnectedness of knowledge and skills that integrate the various strands of the subject.
- I like to teach the whole class, it matches my interaction style as well as my belief that separating pupils by tasks can label them in terms of capability and expectation in a detrimental way.
- I try to design learning tasks that have multiple entry and exit points, which are at least 'open-middle' if not open-ended, so that pupils of differing skill, knowledge and interest levels are engaged, challenged and extended in appropriate ways.
- I encourage children to have input into the direction of enquiries or investigations so that different interests, learning styles and intelligences are taken into account. Children as co-designers of

learning experiences ensure content is meaningful and developmentally appropriate.
• I also believe that what pupils learn is fundamentally connected to how it's learned.

My interpretation of 'learning styles' is that we each have preferred ways of receiving and giving information. Through the experiences they are exposed to, children develop preferences and skills for learning through different modalities, using a favoured sense to gather knowledge and understanding of the world. These ways can be described in three broad categories: visual, auditory and kinaesthetic. In the classroom, informed by my observational assessments of children, I tried to present learning opportunities that took account of each learning style.

Complementary to the notion of variations in receiving and presenting knowledge is Howard Gardner's (1983) explanation of multiple intelligences. The eight intelligences that have been identified represent ways in which learning experiences are processed and indicate how students make sense of and respond to them. Everybody has each of the intelligences available to them, however we tend to utilize and favour one or two over the others. With suitable exposure and teaching, we can strengthen all of our intelligences and expand our learning strategies and capability for being more resourceful. Consequently, we develop a greater capacity for effective problem-solving.

Awareness of learning styles and appreciation of multiple intelligences has broadened the narrow definition I mistakenly held of the mathematically able child as one skilled in computing efficiently and accurately. How about a child able to quickly see and hear a pattern and then extend it? Or the child who identifies spatial relationships more acutely than others; the one who is fast at organizing and rationalizing classifications, or even the verbal child able to infer meaning and detect logical inconsistencies in written problems? Are they less able in mathematics or do they simply bring different skills and talents to bear? In contemplating these questions, I changed my question from 'How (mathematically) intelligent is this child?' to 'How is this child (mathematically) intelligent?'

Even though I had a major goal of being responsive to the emerging interests and need of pupils, I concede that a teacher's work remains central in shaping what goes on in a mathematics class. What students learn about particular concepts and procedures, as well as about thinking mathematically, depends on the ways in which they engage in mathematical activity in their classrooms. The disposition of learners toward mathematics is also shaped by such experiences. Consequently, my goals for developing students' mathematical power and confidence, and for using ICT as part of the process, required careful attention to pedagogy as well as to curriculum content.

The context

The head of the school was very supportive of teachers who tried to improve the programmes they planned and implemented and to develop and expand their teaching methods. Considerable amounts of time and energy had been put into grant writing to support technology initiatives, as well as into ensuring that a substantial proportion of the annual budget went on purchasing computers and related technologies and funding professional development in ICT. To ensure that school-wide technology (for 4- to 12-year-olds in this instance) was introduced and supported in all curriculum areas, a teacher was released from classroom duties to take on the role of technology coordinator. The coordinator had higher degrees in educational technology, was a master teacher and had been a university supervisor of student teachers. She organized and dealt with all administrative requirements to ensure that teachers were able to attend any available continued professional development opportunities and she was prepared to assist or teach any subject, with any age group for a teacher who wanted her support integrating ICT into the curriculum. She had the experiences and attributes to make her an ideal mentor.

The pupils

From their earliest year in school, pupils were familiar with technology being part of their learning environment and the novel effect was not a factor. In their 'upper years', the 60 pupils were taught in two heterogeneous groups by a team of three teachers. The team teaching arrangement was that classes rotated between two adjoining classrooms for different subjects. Two teachers shared responsibility for language arts, health and social science subjects while the third (in this case me) taught mathematics and science. Additionally, there was specialist support for some subjects, including library. All students had one hour of mathematics and of language arts each day alongside other curriculum areas. The weekly schedule included one hour of technology, when specific skills that supported curriculum areas were taught and refined. Over the year each student additionally 'rotated' through a six-week technology course. Technology in this block focused on applying and extending knowledge and technical skills, assembling hardware, installing software and troubleshooting minor problems as well as improving keyboard skills and creating multimedia presentations.

The pupils were economically, socially, ethnically and academically extremely diverse. The levels of attainment represented in the class, as indicated by standardized test scores, varied widely. Scores ranged from a core of children scoring at the 99th percentile to a similar number with scores around the 30th percentile, most of whom had statements of special needs. However, the average level could be summed up as high.

Socioeconomic factors such as home and primary language and access to computers and current technologies also had an impact on performance. What was common to the group was that they were high-spirited, had a disposition to honesty (that is to say, they let you know what activities they did and didn't like) and loved to embark on new learning ventures, especially if computers were involved.

The unit of study

This was my opportunity to risk change and learn if, and how, I could incorporate technology more effectively into the mathematics curriculum so as to enrich the learning experiences for all students. I didn't feel the need to make great claims for originality or creativity for the unit of study. So, after further consideration of the various recommendations and a review of the year's programme, I decided to begin with a unit that I had previously planned and taught. In this way, I would be familiar with the mathematics content and how the work generally evolved and I could turn my attention to other issues. I wanted to focus on using technology right at the beginning of the year and to continue to develop my knowledge and understanding throughout the year.

The first unit I planned to teach, 'Every Picture Tells a Story', focused on data handling and gave the pupils, who arrived from four different classrooms, the opportunity to get to know each other and to track their own changes. It also had cross-curricular links to the health education, language arts and social studies programmes. With some responsive, formative planning around emerging interests, the work could provide meaningful and substantive enquiry, could be driven by the children's essential questions and meet many of the knowledge, skills and performance objectives described for this age group (California State Department of Education 1999). Most importantly, it was open enough to allow pupils of widely varying mathematical skills, interests and learning styles to be actively engaged. It seemed a perfect choice.

The equipment

I took stock of the technologies that were readily accessible:

- 18 computers with the installed package of software (if I shared machines with the teacher in the interconnecting room).
- Every computer was online.
- A 27in wall-mounted TV/VCR with 'Infocus' hook-up for computer display.
- A scanner.
- Email addresses for all pupils.
- A classroom set of calculators.

- Access to two digital cameras.
- An old but functioning Polaroid camera.
- A school video camera that could be borrowed.
- Four audio cassette recorders.
- A wide variety of measuring tools.

I was well resourced! I didn't know how to use some of the software (or hardware) but would experiment beforehand and knew I could arrange for the technology coordinator to come and demonstrate to the whole class and myself how to use the programs as needed. The pupils had been using computers at school for several years and many had computer access and experience outside of school. They could act as peer tutors in their areas of expertise and I could rely on them to teach me. I thought about the technical and mathematical proficiencies of many of the pupils – for example:

- word-processing experience and enviable typing speeds;
- familiarity with sending email messages;
- some spreadsheet knowledge of entering information and using simple formula from a previous unit of study;
- experiences with collecting, organizing and representing data sets;
- ability to measure and convert between simple units of measurement;
- competency in using all four operations with whole numbers, with limited understanding of computing fractional quantities;
- skills in using a variety of tools for linear, mass and angle measures;
- experience in using calculators, which were daily maths tools.

I listed the various steps and stages that I anticipated arising during the unit and considered which of the available technologies we might use to support the work (see Table 7.1). The purpose was to anticipate what needs might arise and to ensure that the mechanics were in place and functioning, and that any human resources I needed to call on were forewarned. Once this was put into a table I felt very nervous. Where was the maths! I knew where it was, but I couldn't see it. For my own peace of mind, I did a task analysis – if the pupils are to engage in a task, what would they need to know, do or learn? I then added in the mathematics (in italics, Table 7.1) and felt much better. However, although my list seemed fairly extensive at the onset, it would turn out to be woefully incomplete.

Every picture tells a story

To introduce the work I spent the last weeks of the summer break online finding interesting or puzzling photographs and pictures. This introduction made an interesting segue into the unit of study. What story did we create in looking at the pictures? What story were they trying to tell? How well did our stories match that intended by the photographers and creators? (see Figure 7.1).

Table 7.1   Planning for anticipated technology use

Stages in the research process	Supporting technologies
Children's participation in planning and designing the work	Email
Writing unambiguous research questions; classifying questions *Examining survey questions and applying logic in critiquing them*	Word processing
Declaring assumptions, forming and communicating hypotheses *Applying logic and communicating mathematically*	Word processing
Designing data collection process *Tallying; drawing matrices*	Emails, databases
Pilot study, reviewing and revising initial question and methods *Applying logical thinking*	Tables, word processing, photocopying
Collection data *Measuring; applying 4 operations to decimals and fractions*	Emails, databases, video and tape recordings, photographs, field notes
Collating data *Looking for patterns, frequencies; constructing graphs; measuring circles; using measures of central tendency*	Spreadsheets, frequency table editing tapes and notes, scanner
Analysing and synthesizing data *Finding distributions and range; interpreting and analysing graphs; making inferences*	Calculators, spreadsheets, drawing tables and graphs
Summarizing findings *Calculating percentages, ratios; applying logical thinking*	Word processing
Modelling the average student *Measuring; constructing models*	Spreadsheets, tables, calculators
Reporting results *Developing a mathematical vocabulary and communicating precisely and mathematically*	Draw and paint programs, written and oral reports, digital photographs, videotapes, video clips, PowerPoint presentations
Comparing and validating results	Research on web
Constructing comparison graphs; applying knowledge of percentage and ratio	Comparison graphs and tables

I found several interesting and quite different graphs on the Internet, in magazines and newspapers. What stories were they telling us? Again, the idea was to compare our personal interpretations with the messages these mathematical pictures were intended to convey (see Figure 7.2). How accurately do mathematical pictures describe data?

This led to one of the children bringing in identikit pictures as examples of inaccurate and ambiguous portrayals of data (see Figure 7.3). The ideas expressed about police enquiry and interpretation moved the children's thinking in the direction of psychological profiles, *Cracker* style. Each child wrote an anonymous self-description and these were distributed, and using Faces (www.facesinterquest.com), a program that a parent had come across, identikit-style pictures were created and then attempts were made to match them with the real person. This was when the students really took over the unit of study. They wanted to know if they could describe

Figure 7.1   What do you think thiswoman is doing?
What evidence do you have to support your interpretation?

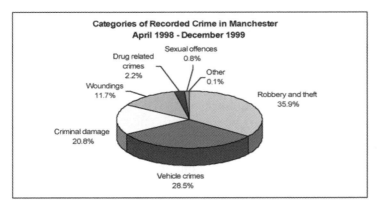

Figure 7.2   What story does this pie chart tell us?
Source: Identikit. www.wbaifree.org/radiofreeeireann/wanted.html

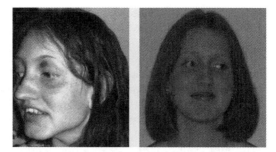

Figure 7.3   Would you have arrested the woman on the right if you had to identify her using the identikit-style picture of the suspect, on the left?

Source: Home Office, Research Development Statistics. www.homeoffice.gov.uk/rds/index.htm

the average sixth-grade student in our school, if they could produce an identikit picture, if there was a physical and psychological profile of an 'average' 11- or 12-year-old they could identify with. The youngsters thought it very significant to be the first class leaving the school in the new millennium. They wanted to capture a snapshot of what adolescents at the turn of the century were like, plus they wanted to be able to keep the information – a personal historical record for when they 'grew up'.

To give structure to the work the children decided they would call the project 'Meet the Class of 2000'. The idea of establishing a data bank about students in the leaving class of the University Elementary School in the year 2000 had high appeal for all of us. It allowed for a group profile, from which statistical averages could be determined and against which children could compare themselves. Essential questions? The pupils thought so. Mathematical inquiry? Certainly. Would technology have a purpose, would it make a substantive difference? I hoped so.

Using ICT in learning and using mathematics

The pupils began by generating questions that they were interested in finding the answers to. These related to their pasts, their own early years and their personal family histories, momentous historical events, preferences, opinions about social issues, what fashions the students followed, predictions for future environmental issues and possible inventions, as well as their personal and physical characteristics. This brainstorming activity became quite a social event, taking place during break, when journeying to and from school, during the after-school programme and over the telephone. Enthusiastically, though hastily, written lists were brought to class, compared, and favourites chosen. I particularly liked 'If you could change your age would you: turn younger, stay the same age, become older?' Such decisions for 11-year-olds!

Children recorded why they were interested in their selected question, whether they had a hypothesis they were seeking to confirm, what answers they anticipated and whether the findings would be used to initiate or inform possible further inquiry. Questions were written on index cards and sorted as to whether they would inform (a) the psychological profile or (b) the physical description. Similar questions were clustered and classified. As pupils considered the types of responses that might be given to the questions, they realized that the question asked determined the answer received. Questions were labelled as 'closed', 'open' or 'forced choice' and the problems and benefits associated with each were hotly but thoughtfully discussed.

A decision was made to focus initially on physical description. To ensure that the questions were all different, the class split into editing groups. Each pupil emailed members of their group with their chosen question and feedback on the clarity and appropriateness was given. Duplicates were replaced and revisions began.

Addressing each of those emails and repeating the same messages soon became tedious. Having spoken at home about the problems she had encountered, one student suggested to the two classes her father's idea of setting up a 'nickname' or alias for each work group. The idea was adopted and the classes set about deciding the most efficient way of entering each member's email address. A designated 'group postmaster' was sent mail from which addresses were cut and pasted into the appropriate fields and shared with other members. Spurred on by what they saw as a more efficient way to manage the flow of information the children embarked on a quest for further ways to streamline sending and receiving data. Using the Eudora manual, some volunteers looked for other possibilities. Nicknames for sub-groups were compiled into a class nickname, after which quick recipient lists, canned messages, attaching questionnaires and setting up mailbox folders to help organize incoming responses all followed quickly.

There was a flurry of linear and mass measurement activity. This was quickly halted as it was realized that consensus needed to be reached about which measurement system to use (this was the US remember, where imperial measures are still in everyday use). Debates about relative benefits gave rise to the decision to use metric, as operating with 'dreadful decimals' was overwhelmingly preferred to using 'frightful fractions', (as they were described by the opposing groups). I was able to sit on the sidelines as the debate proceeded and listen to wonderful explanations, reasoning and defences for each system. I also knew there were going to be plenty of upcoming opportunities to work with 'frightful fractions' regardless of the decision to use the metric system.

The rapidly growing data set led to discussion about how to manage and handle the data as well as discovering the functions of, and methods to, calculate range, distributions and deviations. The data was the vehicle that led to the need to acquire the concepts and learn the skills.

If necessity is the mother of invention, then labour must be the father of discovery. A fortuitous discovery came from a group of students tired of repeating the same information and with peers who lost sets of measurements and responses. Opening up AppleWorks they found the database program. Looking at the dialog boxes that appeared, and with a little experimenting, pupils saw the potential of this tool for sorting and locating information. Most importantly, between us we were able to figure out how to go about setting up the database records. This was quite a breakthrough – we were beginning to take charge of our own learning and it was *cause célèbre* enough for us to have a self-congratulatory party.

After the celebration, we connected a computer to a TV monitor and set up our database. Jointly the pupils decided on the fields of information; and one pupil acted as recorder and entered the field names. This computer was designated 'the information centre' where each student created their personal record for the database. Further repetition was eliminated as 'field type' options were investigated and another short cut was uncovered as popup fields and radio buttons were mastered. The choices for the fields were entered and pupils simply clicked male or female; glasses or no glasses; braces on your teeth or not; eye, hair and skin colour; which subject they preferred to study; and so on. 'This is great for forced choice responses but it's not going to work for open questions,' remarked one pupil. How true!

To assist in data collection for open-ended questions, responses were tape-recorded and when it was felt necessary, Polariod photographs taken. This helped children who might be hampered by limited writing skills. It prevented frustration from getting in the way of participation. Other pupils preferred to gather open and forced choice responses by carefully constructed surveys.

Calculators were found and used, spreadsheets were set up in Excel and mean averages found. A subject of discussion was the relative merits of which technology was more effective versus more efficient for calculating averages. Peer tutoring on spreadsheet use ensured that the choice was available to all pupils. We started out with the most basic of formats, but as soon as a new 'discovery' was made, 'basic' was no longer acceptable. Fonts were changed, colour added and graphs strategically placed on the spreadsheet. All tips and tricks were explored and incorporated until the visual impact was deemed satisfactory. Rather than instruct pupils as to the appropriate information and labels charts should carry, the students generated their own list. Evaluating the use of Excel, students who had constructed surveys recognized that a spreadsheet could have eased the earlier processes of data collection, sorting and tallying.

How representative was the information about our 60 pupils of this age group? To establish if our average student was truly average and to substantiate their claims, pupils emailed and telephoned experts including those at the university and local colleges, paediatricians, psychologists and even local video and food stores. As a result, a brain researcher visited the classroom to speak about changes in brain capacity during adolescence. Fascinating stuff! This visit was followed by a sociologist researching play in older children. We heard how professional researchers work and about her own findings. She heard about kids' play and had more data. Everybody was a winner.

We graduated to the Internet. At first, it was difficult for the children to locate the information they were hoping to find. We discussed how information might be found if they were using print sources. One pupil visited the library and asked the librarian for assistance. She came to the classroom and demonstrated key word searches and how to refine searches using Boolean logic. Data was gathered from sociological survey reports, US population data provided national and local demographics and *USA Today*'s *Teen Survey* described physical characteristics of same-age youngsters.

Kids Count, a project of the Annie E. Casey Foundation, was a website that provided information from the US census for 2000 that impacted children's lives. In addition to providing state and national statistics in its data book section, pupils could select the form in which they wanted to have the findings presented (see Figure 7.4). This was a wonderful opportunity to examine the functions, uses and merits of different forms of data display. A homework assignment was to find examples of the various forms either on the web or in printed material, to be brought to class with an interpretation of the data. Every picture was indeed telling a story.

By this stage the students were so engrossed in their work that they had to sign on a rota to stay in during free time. There was some straying from the task and minor indiscretion in using the computers, but the 'appropriate and responsible computer use' contracts the technology coordinator insisted each pupil sign, as well as a parent or guardian, were taken very seriously. The information gathered via the Internet was used as pupils wrote up their findings, conclusions and recommendations for further study. Energized by their own results, the pupils decided to make their own sociological statement.

Figure 7.4   The Kids Count website gives options for the way the selected data is presented

Source: Kids Count, Annie E. Casey Foundation, Baltimore. www.aecf.org/termsofuse.htm

Using ICT to communicate mathematical pictures

There was much brainstorming concerning possible ways to display findings effectively. There was also the recognition that a variety of formats would add interest for the audience, giving rise to discussion of who comprised the audience and what was meant by 'appropriate presentation'. The initial inclination was to focus solely on drawing bar charts, histograms and pie charts – after all, this *was* mathematics. I brought to class some examples of how information was reported: audiotaped news reports, *USA Today*'s daily graphs and charts, advertisements from magazines, television video clips and the original work of a graphic artist. The technology coordinator then demonstrated and taught us how to use the PowerPoint application. This opened up the possibilities of how children chose to communicate their mathematical message to an audience by using ICT.

With little prompting, plans were soon underway for:

- books and broadsheets, including a class newsletter, to be written and illustrated (see Figure 7.5);
- movies and videos to be made and edited;
- digital photographs to be taken to record this moment in time;
- mock news reports and 'documentaries' to be presented, complete with film and computer support;
- PowerPoint presentations to be designed and assembled (see Figure 7.6).

Each presentation included the ubiquitous bar charts, histograms and pie charts. Multiple ways of 'showing what you know' were evident and the suggestions and choices revealed a great deal about the learning styles and talents of the children.

'Who do you think is most like the average student?' had seemed a simple enough question at the time it was asked. Within minutes, the search was on. This was the opportunity to consider measures of central tendency, their purpose and validity. Could we even determine if there was an average 'name'? One student had found 'the Table menu' on the menu bar and experimented with its use. She taught this tool to both class groups. What was most appreciated was the easy way it assisted in alphabetical sorting, a boon when modal averages were introduced.

The database was the stimulus for one group to 'build' a life-sized model of the average student. With a modest amount of hinting I was able to introduce the idea of making a scale model to a second group. This provided a challenge for some of the higher-skilled members of the class, who then peer tutored the rest of their group in rounding decimals, deciding on a scale and making the appropriate and necessary calculations. Quite a number of class members were up to their necks in making papier mâché models. It was the perfect opportunity to have them describe how they were using estimation skills, a variety of measures and tools (including callipers and scaled rulers), and what they were learning about ratio,

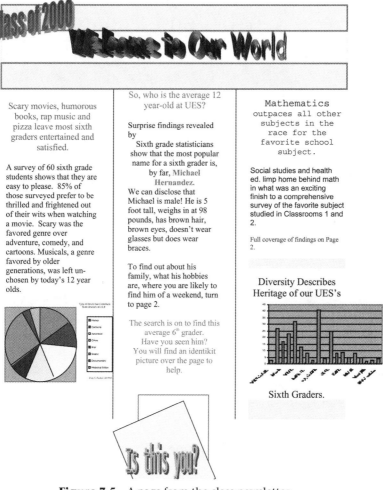

Figure 7.5 A page from the class newsletter

proportion and calculating scale. Another group decided to utilize their word-processing skills and love of language arts to write a description of this statistical mystery character. A further group took digital photographs for their exhibition, 'Life and Times of A Sixth Grader', to show how close to, or different from, the average 'model student' members of the class were (see Figure 7.7).

If all of this sounds as though we had strayed away from the mathematical underpinning of the unit, be assured that we hadn't. Quite the opposite: mathematics was all over the curriculum at this point – in language arts, health education, art and the library. Mathematics was even

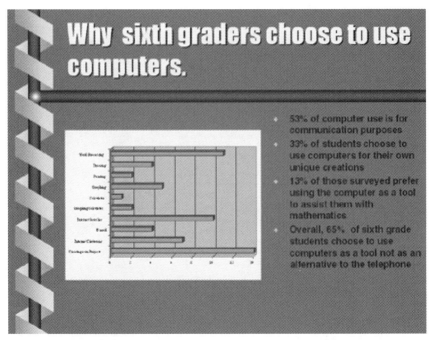

Figure 7.6 A class-constructed PowerPoint presentation

in drama where two student teachers were making movies with two groups of pupils, and in music, with one group writing a 'rap' song of their findings and using an electronic keyboard to add the music.

Showcasing the work

The year group was scheduled to display work in the main hallway of school. Mathematics work was relatively under-represented and this was a chance to right the balance. Having recently examined the impact of advertising posters, the pupils decided that a display of posters would be an effective way to get their mathematical information across to a wider audience within the school community and to visitors. This was also a medium for getting some community involvement in mathematics and to show cross-curricular links meaningfully. A colleague knew a graphic artist who was prepared to give two input sessions to the classes on elements of communicative, eye-catching and easy to read posters, and to give feedback on the pupils' computer-generated drafts.

Designing and setting the layout was a surprising application of maths skills. Proportions of text blocks to graphics were calculated, proportions were converted to percentages of the poster paper, percentage areas of

Michael Evan Hernandez: The Average Kind of Guy

A construction project finished December 8th, 1999
by
Classroom 1, Class of 2000!

We have made an average sort of student using the data collected from all of the students of the Class of 2000. We measured ourselves for the width and height of our limbs, the torso, necks and heads. We entered all of the information onto a spreadsheet and the average sizes were calculated for us. Some people did not trust the computer to do the calculations (or themselves to use it!) and used calculators and paper and pencil to do the job. We even found averages for shoe sizes (the Fila shoes the model student is wearing aren't the 'average' brand shoe). This average differed from the mean average we found for measurements, it was the modal average which tells us information about the most popular, common or fashionable data that is not reported as a number or quantity. Using modes we were able to discover the most common hair and eye color, shirt and pants size, his birthday, hobbies and favorite lesson. 'HE' because we have a ratio of 10:3 boys to girls in one of the classes this year! Michael was the most common name, with two in each of the classrooms. We also had two Justins and two Evans. So we surveyed the classes and found that three people had Michael as their middle name - that made it official. I have given Michael the middle name of Evan because that's my name, and I wanted to make a decision. 'H' is most definitely the most common initial letter for last names. We had two Hernandez and two Hochheims, but the Hochheims are twins, so the class voted on Hernandez - it is not very mathematical but it is democratic.

The construction of the 'model student' was quite difficult, because we did a lot of arguing about jobs and some people were not very responsible. Mr. Castro helped us collect the materials together and we found time to measure, build, paint and glue during break, lunch and in some class time too. We are very pleased with the results and some people want to keep Michael as a reminder of our last year in UES and how we looked (on average). Nobody in the class looks like Michael, we are all happy about that. Michael is proof that averages are like pictures that help tell stories, they are helpful but not always real and we should not expect to find them anywhere.

Again, all of the physical attributes are the average of all the students in the class.

By: *Evan H. and Alex F.*

Figure 7.7   One group's description of 'The Average Kind of Guy'

the paper were measured and blocked off. Once the mathematics was completed, to enliven and strengthen the message of the posters, some pupils wanted to add photographs. This necessitated them learning how to download and edit digital photographs and insert them into their documents. Other students wanted to scan hand-drawn graphs to use in the posters, add captions and alter and align the pictures. Combinations of paint and draw programs were used and Adobe Pagemaker was introduced. Images from the web were imported and resized and each student gathered images to build their own 'clipart' library for future use. Word-processing skills were honed and increased and mathematical vocabulary was employed and fine-tuned as data were distilled to convey the important findings (see Figure 7.8). Throughout the exercise there were constant reminders that the purpose was to communicate and give life to a mathematical message.

As they worked and I listened to their conversations and responded to their questions and comments, I saw learners who were fully immersed with complete mental, as well as physical active, engagement. They were being challenged to think and communicate mathematically as they struggled to choose mathematical vocabulary that conveyed their ideas, procedures and findings. The technology was being used for both information and communication – it was media by which they could explore and investigate mathematical concepts and develop and reinforce their skills. There had been no textbooks and very few worksheets; the learning had not been passive or vicarious but was initiated and sustained by the students' own interests and inquiries.

This was a powerful culminating activity. The posters were carefully hung in the main hall, and a school T-shirt clad model of 'Michael Hernandez' was seated close by. At the touch of a button, the video 'Meet the Class of 2000' played on a borrowed combination TV/VCR unit. Were mathematical messages being effectively communicated through ICT? The evidence suggested a resounding 'Yes'. Seeing so many people in the hallway reading their posters, amused by the ever-vigilant model of 'Michael Hernandez' and watching the video with interest and admiration proved to be a great confidence booster and source of pride to all the pupils.

Evaluating progress

The project had taken on a life of its own and I was getting nervous that we were about to enter the sixth week and still had a way to go. I felt the need to justify the time spent. I was more confident about the technology than the mathematics skills and knowledge being developed, but that was probably a reflection of my own growth.

To calm my nerves, I listed the mathematical content and processes (see Tables 7.2 and 7.3) along with the technology skills (see Table 7.4) set out in the school's internal document, which was an amalgam of external curricular frameworks. I had never considered the document to be a prescription for practice but I did consider that I had an obligation to try to ensure that pupils covered what the school had agreed to. The task was a useful way to assess if and what goals were being met. At a glance I could see that the classes were covering an incredible amount

Question
What is your favorite type of food?

Research Statement

I was interested in finding out the favorite types of food of the sixth grade class of 2000. I didn't set out with a hypothesis to prove, but wondered if young people preferred fast foods.

Method of Data Collection

On December 7, 1999 I collected my data. I did this by going around with a class list for rooms one and two. I asking 30 people, individually, my open question(What is your favorite type of food?) I marked their answers on the class list. After surveying 30 people, my data collection was complete. The sample group was 50% of the sample set and sufficient to get reliable results.

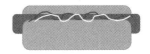

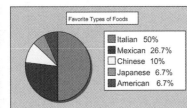

Favorite Types of Foods	
Italian	50%
Mexican	26.7%
Chinese	10%
Japanese	6.7%
American	6.7%

How the information was organized

I organized the information by adding the number of responses given in each of the five food choice categories to find out how many people liked each type of food.
From my data, I found the percentages for the choices and then calculated how many degrees each section would be on my pie chart. I decided to make a pie chart starting with the biggest percentage. I also made a bar graph. Organizing the information on easy to 'read' graphs and charts made it easy to understand and interpret.

These computer generated graphs represent the ones that I drew.

Findings

I discovered that 50% of the respondents prefered Italian food, 26% liked Mexican, 10% liked Chinese, 7% liked Japanese, and 7% liked American food. Half of the 6th grade respondents like Italian food and a little more than one fourth like Mexican. I think that people like Italian food more because most people's favorite food is pizza. Also, I think Mexican food is popular because we live near Mexico and have authentic, good tasting Mexican food. This means that one quarter of the pie chart shows 3 other types of food: Chinese, Japanese and American. These are my unquestionable findings on sixth graders' favorite types of foods. I believe people's tastes will vary depending on the cultural make up of the city they live in.

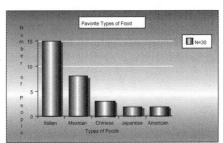

Conclusion

The sixth grade class of 2000's favorite type of food is absolutely Indian food.

Suggestion for further inquiry

A further study could survey every grade level at UCS and see if students favorite types of foods changes at each grade.

By Ben *****
1-5-00

Figure 7.8   The 'Favorite Types of Foods' poster

Table 7.2 Mapping mathematical content

Mathematics strand	Match with formal frameworks	Match with school's math standards
Number and operations	Acquires fluency in basic skills Demonstrates understanding of place value, ordering and rounding Acquires and applies skills with fractions, decimals, percentages, ration and proportion Uses decimal notatio for tenths, hundredths and thousandths when recording measurements and in calculations Expresses a quotient as a fraction or as a decimal	Uses four operations accurately on integers, common and decimal fractions and percents Finds equivalent forms between common, decimal fractions and percents Appropriately expresses answers as common, decimal fractions or percents
Data handling, statistics and probability	Analyses evidence and builds arguments to support or refute hypotheses Shows understanding of ways data are gathered and presented in graphs, diagrams, tables and charts Collects discrete and continuous data Solves problems by representing, inferring, extracting and interpreting data and predicting from it Finds the mean, mode and median and range of a set of data Understands difference between measures of central tendency and purpose for which each is used Begins to find the median and mean of a set of data	Constructs surveys: designs appropriate question, collates and interprets data Understands different forms of questions and their purpose Displays data accurately using appropriate form of graph for its function Predicts from data set Uses sample space to describe the possibility of an event Calculates and uses appropriate measure of central tendency
Measurement	Uses, reads and writes standard metric units including their abbreviations, and relationships between them Converts smaller to larger units of measure and vice versa Suggests suitable units and measuring equipment to estimate or measure length, mass and capacity Appreciates concept of scale Understands and works with ratio and proportion and uses proportional reasoning to solve problems	Measures and records precisely, uses metric/imperial measures accurately Reads and interprets scales on various measuring instruments Converts accurately between units of measurement Able to apply four operations to units of measurement

Table 7.3 Mapping mathematical processes

Mathematical process	Match with formal frameworks	Match with school's math standards
Problem-solving	Chooses and applies appropriate strategy to solve mathematics and everyday life problems Solves problems involving 'real life', money or measures	Applies a variety of strategies to effectively solve problems
Reasoning and proof	Analyses evidence and builds arguments to support or refute hypotheses Is able to use reasoning to solve mathematical problems Explains relationships, generalizes and predicts	Is able to prove validity of answer or idea Recognizes differences between opinions, assumptions and facts
Connections	Makes connections among mathematical ideas and between mathematics and other disciplines	Is able to find connections between mathematical ideas and procedures and to use that insight to solve new problems Generalizes from specific events or answers
Communication	Explains methods and reasoning, orally and in writing Uses the vocabulary of estimation and approximation Communicates precisely about quantities and relationships Uses the language associated with probability to discuss events, including those with equally likely outcomes Communicates interpretations and results of a statistical inquiry Uses selected tables, graphs, models and diagrams in support of explanations of mathematical reasoning	Composes different forms of questions to match their purpose Displays data accurately using appropriate form of graph or table for its function Redefines problems to show understanding of task
Representation	Uses a variety of signs, symbols, models, graphs and mathematical terms to communicate precisely Uses informal pencil and paper methods to support, record or explain Draws frequency tables, bar chart tables, graphs and diagrams, including those generated by a computer	Clearly and confidently explains reasoning and procedures in a variety of written, symbolic or verbal forms

Table 7.4 Mapping technology skills

Technology	Match with formal frameworks	Match with school's math standards
Calculators	Uses calculator to solve problems Uses calculator to check answers	Uses calculator proficiently and effectively Demonstrates understanding of the math process the calculator is being used for Is able to judge when calculator use is appropriate and efficient
Computers	Understands the mathematical skills, concepts and relationships behind the purpose of the tools Uses electronic tools to extend comprehension, reasoning and problem-solving skills beyond what is possible with traditional resources	Can operate effectively a variety of machines Recognizes a computer as a tool for improving learning, productivity and performance Can assess and fix minor problems Demonstrates age-appropriate level of keyboard skills
Software	Is familiar with the purpose and function of a variety of general software and selects from them prudently Uses databases to store, organize and access information Keys in information to spreadsheets, produces graphs and compiles statistics Uses technology to express mathematical ideas precisely.	Uses a variety of appropriate, available software packages to assist and enhance learning Can import and export images and text between applications Is able to enhance work with draw and paint programs Uses database and spreadsheet software to manage and retrieve information Can teach others to use software Is familiar with use of Adobe Print and Photoshop in enhancing images Can scan and edit pictures and text
Digital resources	Exchanges ideas and tests hypotheses with a wide audience Recognizes and applies mathematics in contexts outside of mathematics	Conducts research through the stages of information management Evaluates information gathered Uses information to create new knowledge Is able to use digital imaging equipment to download and edit images
Multimedia	Communicates mathematical thinking coherently and clearly through presentation media	Identifies a variety of resources from which to collect information, including people, technology, the web, electronic encyclopedias and databases, places and print Presents what they have learned through a variety of presentation modes (e.g. drama, written reports, storytelling and multimedia presentations that use Hyper-Studio or PowerPoint)

of material, exceeding what would usually be covered in the time. Much of the material in fact formed the core of a more advanced programme of study.

While I had a sense of accomplishment in terms of coverage, I was very aware of the range of abilities, skills and interests among the students. Were all pupils fully engaged and challenged in appropriate ways? Was individual growth being achieved and maximized?

The pupils had been selected for work groups that would represent a range of learning styles, intelligences to be shared, and talents and interests that would complement others in the group. The class operated on a cooperative learning model, group goals were set and tasks were divided. Each person was held responsible for contributing to the final product and members shared their expertise and taught others the skills needed to accomplish tasks. Everybody had the opportunity, and indeed was expected, to contribute. Language skills were extended and developed in a non-threatening situation, an important consideration because of second-language learners within the classes. The room was busy and noisy, but it was focused on the work and the general atmosphere was that of a high-energy learning environment.

Because everybody was independently involved in exploring and using the technology, I was able to get to every group each lesson. I could offer support, hear and assess needs, provide suggestions, reinforce expectations, gain insights and keep informed about how individuals were performing. As a result, I could call the whole class together to discuss issues that arose, give instruction in procedures and have groups share findings and technology 'discoveries'. I could also pull small groups for tutoring or to preview upcoming instruction. I had pupils make frequent self-assessments of what they were learning and what skills they were developing or applying and practising.

Without a doubt, my planning, guidance and facilitation of the work could have been reordered and streamlined. But the way the study emerged and evolved was as teaching and learning in the context of needing and wanting to acquire knowledge and further understanding. I was able to be responsive to what I observed, to emerging interests, as well as the work I received and could make adjustments or additions accordingly. Being responsive included introducing a topic or a new piece of technology equipment, consulting with or bringing in one of our 'expert' resources or alternatively not introducing new topics or technology until a more timely opportunity, based on my observations. But the most valuable evaluation came from the data the pupils collected. They were providing what I needed so that I could ensure the work was meeting their needs.

As parts of the overall project were completed, I assessed new learning. There were three required products: a page for the 'Meet the Class of 2000' book, a presentation of the group findings to be made to the whole class and a poster summarizing and displaying our findings. These were more authentic forms of assessment than setting a 'test' would be. As the measure of success was the clear communication of a mathematical message to an audience, the class evaluated the presentations on previously decided criteria. This way, they had a cognitive map of what an effective presentation should include. Each presentation was video-taped so that groups could view and critique their own performances. The audience completed evaluation sheets, which were immediately returned so that feedback was instant. The group could then discuss what went well and what future changes could be made, and the onus was not on any individual in terms of how the group presentation was received.

In terms of the objective of infusing mathematics learning with technology, based on the learning climate, this was a most successful venture. The quality of the final products was variable though generally good and without doubt each child made his or her best effort and portrayed talents and skills to best effect. In an uncontrived way, a very wide range of technologies had been employed. Technology use had definitely been driven by pupil need and enthusiasm. At the onset of this 'experiment' I had never anticipated as much equipment could have been so appropriately integrated.

The pupils made a summative evaluation of the unit of study. Now it was my turn to collect, compile and analyse the data (see Figure 7.9). I used the results to determine what new skills pupils believed they had acquired, how they were able to apply new and existing skills to their work and to assess their levels of engagement during the unit of study. The results left me in no doubt that in future I would integrate technology into each unit of the mathematics curriculum. The children reported positive affects in all regards; they felt more engaged in learning and thought they had learned more than in the conventional delivery of the mathematics curriculum. The technology skills acquired were seen to be generalizable to other curriculum areas.

The end of the beginning

David Thornberg (1999) optimistically wrote:

> I've felt that the reluctant educators would come around in time, especially as the technology improved to the point where the advantages were obvious. And, while it is true that many educators are finding computers and telecommunications to be useful in the classroom, there are still many who resist any attempt to bring technologies into the classroom that are found in roughly half of America's homes. And, in some cases, educational technology that does make it to the classroom sits underutilized because the teachers have not been provided with the staff development they need to use these tools effectively.

Please think about the questions carefully.
They require different types of answers.

As always, honest responses are the most useful because they will
help improve your math classes for the rest of the year.

➤ What new mathematics have <u>you</u> learned during this unit of study?

➤ I enjoyed the work I have done.

➤ I felt as though I learned a great deal during the unit

➤ Have you used existing math knowledge and skills in different ways?

➤ Are there any ways this math unit has been different from your usual work?

➤ What new ICT skills have <u>you</u> acquired during this unit of study?

➤ Have you used existing ICT knowledge and skills in different ways?

➤ Which technology (hardware and/or software) do <u>you</u> think added most to the math you were learning? Explain your choice.

➤ Which technology do <u>you</u> think <u>you</u> will use again in learning mathematics?

Figure 7.9   Student evaluation survey

The principal sent a clearly articulated message that teachers were expected to, and would be assisted in, transforming their practice and that action research would heighten teachers' awareness of the process and the pain of change. Her message went beyond rhetoric: Thornberg's idea of teachers being provided with adequate support and ongoing access to professional development in order to release the full potential of technology as an effective teaching tool was given form:

- substantial financial resources were committed to provision;
- there was provision of a full-time ICT coordinator, freed from classroom responsibility and therefore available to offer guidance and tutoring when needed;
- sufficient technology was provided to enable teachers to access equipment easily;
- provision of in-service opportunities that allowed teachers exposure to new and significant ideas was organized and scheduled into the year's programme.

The technology coordinator described some of the ways she provides critical leadership and works alongside staff to provide professional assistance and stimulating ideas about the potential for technology use:

> Individual teachers can acquire technology integration assistance with one-on-one planning, modelling and co-teaching of instruction with the technology coordinator. Also, voluntary mini-workshops are designed to meet the needs identified by an annual 'Technology Use' survey that each teacher completes to appraise their growth and set personal goals about how and what they would like to accomplish in technology integration. We can arrange four two-hour sessions during the school year. Alternatively, teachers develop their technology skills and thinking with whole-school instruction (e.g. use of email); or by attending national or local conferences.

As well as the culture, the organizational structure of the school was a supporting mechanism. Classroom teachers are all too aware that the timetable too often drives the curriculum. To be able to deliver a programme that interfaces with all other areas of the curriculum requires flexible timetabling and large time blocks for teaching and team teaching practices. The opportunity to talk with colleagues, ask their advice and learn together is vital.

While it is important to develop some mastery of computers and communication technologies if teachers are to guide pupils in their effective use, developing skills in a vacuum does nothing to ensure better mathematics teaching or establish a more rigorous curriculum. Not only do you have to plan what technology might enhance the mathematics pupils engage with, but curriculum development, evaluation and revision must take into account the mathematical opportunities provided by the technology. Emphasis must be placed on the use of technology to teach mathematical concepts, skills and applications in the way they are encountered in an age of ever-increasing access to more powerful technology.

Infusing technology into mathematics did not necessitate a significant departure from some of the more traditional practices of working with youngsters as they learn mathematics. It did however suggest changes, not only to what was taught but also to how it was taught. Both the teachers and students assumed different roles and the enterprise gave rise to different notions about what it means to know and to do mathematics. The sum effect was to create a community of learners.

Curriculum decisions are ultimately made to improve the learning experiences of students. What were the gains for the pupils in this case? The work added to their experiences of using ICT in the learning and application of mathematics and in communicating a mathematical message to an audience. What was facilitated was an opportunity to engage in mathematics in a discrete way as well as experiencing how mathematics integrates with other learning opportunities. Data collection and statistics content was an appropriate vehicle for the integration of technology. The inquiries and questions generated by the students were likely to bring about learning that was real in that they set out to gather what they considered to be 'essential' information. Meaningfulness gave rise to high levels of pupil involvement and produced an energized atmosphere for learning. Understandings of mathematics and technology were broadened and deepened in ways that the pupils are more likely to encounter in the era of information and creativity. Using ICT to solve genuine problems demanded higher-level thinking, exploration and creativity to handle the data and publicly communicate the findings. Because the pupils' acquisition of technology know-how and mathematical procedures was needs driven and because practice was achieved through using and representing the same knowledge and skills in different contexts, I believe that their learning was more authentic and hopefully will prove to be more enduring.

I have broken through a personal barrier of resistance and have passed the point of regarding computers and communication technologies as an added burden to the mathematics curriculum. I have moved beyond using technology as an entertaining, decorative toy, a token to modernism, to a place where I regard it as a valuable, resourceful and integral tool. I am not prepared to allow children to leave the first stage of their schooling without gaining mastery in basic lifelong skills of mathematics, nor should I be prepared to deprive them of ICT proficiency. I am encouraged enough to be thinking of ways to redesign each unit of study that I teach to incorporate ICT. I am not able to enumerate a set of concrete skills for effective technology use in mathematics education in my idiosyncratic classroom, but I have passed the starting point.

Finding a meaningful purpose and place for technology in the primary mathematics curriculum is part of a personal journey of discovery. The road travelled so far has been part of a journey that will clearly be endless for me as an educator. Along the way, I have been able to take learning excursions and admire the scenery without being diverted from the destination point – preparing my pupils for their futures.

References

California State Department of Education (1999) *Mathematics Content Standards for California Public Schools (K-12)*. Sacramento, CA: California Department of Education. www.cde.ca.gov/cdepress/standards-pdfs/mathematics.pdf

California State Department of Education (2000) *Mathematics Framework for California Public Schools (K-12)*. Sacramento, CA: California Department of Education. www.cde.ca.gov/cdepress/math.pdf

DfEE (Department for Education and Employment) (1999) *The National Numeracy Strategy: Framework for Teaching Mathematics from Reception to Year 6*. Cambridge: Cambridge University Press.

Gardner, H. (1983) *Frames of Mind*. New York: Basic Books.

Lortie, D. (1975) *Schoolteacher*. Chicago: Chicago University Press.

NCTM (National Council of Teachers of Mathematics) (2000) *Principles and Standards 2000 for School Mathematics*. http://standards.nctm.org.

Piaget, J-P. (1973) *To Understand is to Invent*. New York: Grossman.

Thornberg, D. (1996) *Redefining Teaching in a Disintermediated World*. http://tcpd.gsn.org

Thornberg, D. (1999) *Converting the Techno-phobic*. www.pbs.org/teachersource/thornberg/thornberg399.shtm

CD-ROMS

Faces: The ultimate composite picture. Fresno, CA: IQ Biometrix. www.iqbiometrix.com/education_faces_in_schools.html

Identikit: Find the face that fits. London: Tivola Electronic Publishing. www.tivola.co.uk

Web resources

The Antique Shop Murder. Stories from the Crime Museum: www.met.police.uk/history/bush.htm

Human Identikit: www.whom.co.uk/idk/idkhuman.html

National Statistics Online: www.statistics.gov.uk

UK Online, government information and services: www.ukonline.gov.uk/Home/HoHome

8
ICT AS A TOOL FOR LEARNING – WHERE ARE WE GOING?

Toni Beardon and Jenni Way

No turning back

A school in the modern world without computers is now almost as disadvantaged as a school without books, and cost considerations are changing. In addition to many software applications available as free downloads – which provide excellent learning environments – many agencies, including governments both local and national, now publish learning resources on the web bringing free and up-to-date curriculum materials to schools that have access to the Internet.

The opening up of classrooms to the world of information through the Internet does not diminish the teacher's role or responsibility. On the contrary the teacher's job is even more important because of the changes brought about by computers in the world outside the school, requiring adults to learn new skills to keep up with the pace of technological change at work and in the home. Schools need to prepare children for their life beyond school and this applies to the first year of school as much as it does for older children. Teachers can show by example what it is to be a good learner, how to learn to use new software, how to find and interpret information and how to be discriminating in selecting material.

Families are buying educational computer games for small children and the television in the living room increasingly gives access to the Internet. Some children are learning by 3 or 4 years' old to switch on the computer, select and open up a software package, manage a mouse, play different educational games and recognize numbers, letters, colours, etc. It is not uncommon to see a child of 4 instructing a younger sibling or friend in all this. If the adults in their lives have made discriminating choices of the learning material, then the children go to school with very high expectations of the learning environments they will find there.

In the twentieth century it was necessary for some people to spend their working lives doing mathematical tasks that have now been taken over by computers. In this century we are empowered by the technology; the challenge for education is to develop those human talents that machines cannot match. The main purpose of learning how to carry out mathematical tasks that machines can do more efficiently is to build an understanding of the underlying mathematics so as to be able to use the machines effectively.

Computers, including handheld technology, now rapidly perform routine but complicated mathematical operations and not just arithmetic. Instrumental teaching, which helps children to get the right answers but not to understand how the processes work, may achieve good examination results but has little educational value. It does not educate children to understand how mathematics is applied, or teach them to use mathematics to solve real problems. It does not help them to appreciate mathematics as human achievement (like art, music or literature) and it does not equip them to use technology intelligently.

There is a school of thought that it may be harmful to allow the use of technology before certain basic skills have been mastered. The serious debate has moved on from when to introduce the use of calculators in mathematics lessons to how to give our pupils the best possible advantage from learning with the new technologies so that they understand mathematical concepts and why the methods work and are proficient in mental arithmetic, leading to fluency with algebra, the language of mathematics. We have the power to learn from exploring mathematics as no generation before has ever had. This is already changing, in exciting ways, how we teach.

In the last 30 years the reasons for teaching and learning mathematical methods, algorithms and procedures that can now be carried out by machine have changed. It is still important to develop 'number sense', skills in mental arithmetic and a facility with algebra. Research has not found a proven way for children to learn these skills and it is still believed that to do so children need repetitive practice in carrying out mechanical mathematical processes (just as it is necessary to practise when learning a musical instrument or as an athlete). This alone is not now sufficient – the ultimate purpose is to give children the power which comes from being able to think intelligently and being able to judge when and how to make appropriate use of technology. Those who have been long in the profession are having to rethink their teaching methods and no one can afford to model their teaching entirely on their experience of good teaching from the past.

Much routine work has been automated and employment opportunities, as well as management of our daily lives, call for people who can readily learn new skills and confidently use computers. Teachers therefore have the unavoidable responsibility to incorporate various technologies into their teaching of mathematics and to keep abreast with new developments. This is a challenge and good teaching also depends on showing pupils by example that learning is enjoyable. Being a professional involves learning throughout one's working life.

Calculators

So how do we as teachers take up the challenge? Looking back at the earlier chapters of this book we now highlight some of the important issues raised and the teaching ideas suggested. It is only natural for teachers who have hitherto had little opportunity to use technology in their teaching, or perhaps just little inclination to do so, when they embark upon using technology to look for ideas that fit into their preferred teaching style. This is a good way to start, and to gain confidence, but if they then move on to vary their teaching they will probably find that, along with their pupils, they gain from the experience and find it satisfying. The practical ideas in this book have already had this effect for teachers who have tried them out.

Teachers have found many different ways to incorporate the use of calculators into their teaching so that the focus remains on developing skills and on understanding mathematics. Teachers need to ask different types of questions when children are using calculators, as suggested in Ruth Forrester's chapter. For example, the question 'Find and record ten different ways to do a calculation which has the answer 24' engages pupils in exploration with calculators and they can work at a variety of levels, everyone experiencing success. Finding the best way to record such calculations may be one of the learning objectives. Pupils get rapid feedback in such experimentation and they can check new ideas before committing themselves. Sharing their findings with the rest of the class can be an incentive to further extend the boundaries of what they know.

If the emphasis is on questioning how and why the answers turn out as they do, and whether answers are roughly what should be expected, then the use of calculators will help children to understand and remember number concepts and properties. Children often encounter and 'discover' negative numbers, standard notation and mathematical functions for themselves from calculator use and this provides an incentive to understand the mathematics involved. Problem-solving activities can be more varied and challenging with the use of calculators to encourage thinking skills and to support concept development.

The graphic calculator's mode of operation and large display allow exploration and discovery of procedures or 'rules' such as order of operations and inverse operations. Graphic calculators can be used to help to lay the foundations for algebraic thinking (using memories). Programs provide outcomes or data for children to investigate, as well as simple statistical analysis of personally collected data and help with connections to spatial representations (graphing), allowing 'visualization' of data and experimentation with scale and different types of graph.

Graphic calculators are now powerful handheld mini-computers that have moved the use of calculators beyond number work to spatial work and data handling, including coordinates, angles, symmetry and data logging. Calculators can be used to support learning as and when appropriate, and for a few minutes or longer as required, allowing teachers to enhance their teaching of any topic at any time rather than having to restrict the use of technology to the times when the computer room is available. The pupil does not have to wait for a turn on the class computer – the handheld device gives everyone time and opportunity to use the technology to assist their learning.

Spreadsheets

Generic spreadsheet software can often be used to enhance the teaching and learning of mathematics. Pat Perks and Stephanie Prestage have introduced simple-to-follow techniques for using spreadsheets with large fonts as on-screen 'flash cards', and for producing clear and visually compelling demonstrations and exercises to support the teaching of topics such as telling the time, fractions, decimals and percentages, number recognition, place value, number sequences, multiplication tables and representing data. They have shown how to set up your own versatile displays and worksheets and how to exploit different number formats, the random number and other functions, and the facility for setting up and quickly copying formulae. As with any teaching resource, teachers need to think about which topics are best suited and how spreadsheets might be used to illustrate or explore the concepts, skills and processes involved. The techniques and ideas explained in Chapter 3 show a variety of uses for spreadsheets and can clearly be extended for teaching other topics.

Sometimes the tool is in the hands of the teacher, as in the production of on-screen flash cards, and sometimes the tool is in the hands of the pupils, as in group problem-solving to work out the necessary 'instructions' for the spreadsheet to carry out the desired mathematical operations. Spreadsheets offer the opportunity for linking visual imagery and spatial representations of number and data, as in producing various forms of graphs and diagrams.

The mathematics remains essentially the same, but the use of spreadsheets adds new dimensions such as speed of calculation, the organization and tabulation of results, the ability to vary numbers quickly and explore lots of calculations simultaneously, plus clarity of recording and representing data.

Technologies for different learning styles

The chapter by John Vincent on learning technologies, learning styles and learning mathematics gives some case studies and a rationale, and references to some of the research evidence for using technology in the mathematics classroom so as to release children to learn in a constructivist mode through discovery and to cater for the different learning styles of the pupils. This does not imply a departure from the curriculum, as John says: 'The teacher still provides the goal. The teacher still offers the challenges'.

In the chapter giving a teacher's perspective on changing her teaching style, Merilyn Buchanan also addresses the ways in which using technology as a tool for learning can accommodate different learning styles. She describes how her pupils engaged in meaningful and substantive mathematics-based inquiry, taking full advantage of the technologies available and learning new mathematics and new technical skills in order to conduct their inquiry and communicate the results. Teaching in this way encourages children to have an input into the direction of inquiries or investigations so that different interests, learning styles and intelligences are taken into account.

Children with different learning needs and learning styles, given access to computers, open-ended software (e.g. Microworlds) and simple problems, often challenge themselves with more and more complex tasks. Teachers can feel threatened in such an open-ended learning environment in which the children take control of their learning, and often develop new ICT skills unfamiliar to the teacher. It takes courage on the part of the teacher to release control and permit real child-centred learning but, when they do, hidden abilities and creativity in the children can be uncovered and the mathematical concept development and thinking often go well beyond the expected outcomes.

Howard Gardiner of Harvard University has advanced the theory that there are multiple forms of intelligence – namely, verbal/linguistic, musical/rhythmic, logical/mathematical, visual/spatial, bodily/kinaesthetic and intrapersonal/interpersonal. While this definition of intelligence remains controversial, it is commonly believed that there are different learning styles and preferences from one individual to another and that some people learn better from certain styles of teaching and others from other styles of teaching.

Appropriate use of technologies gives teachers the power to enhance learning and cater for different learning styles. In order to cater more effectively for individuals without increasing their own burden of checking students' work, teachers can, using computers, select learning exercises for different students according to their learning preferences. Diagnostic assessment and profiling of student progress can be assisted by the computer. It is the norm now for school mathematics textbooks in Australia to incorporate a CD-ROM with assessment tests that give automatic entries of results in the teacher's mark book.

In class, children take part in a whole range of interactions. There is the teacher who organizes their learning activities and answers their questions and there are the groups of children with whom they work. Each child contributes to learning interactions, sometimes as part of a whole class, at other times in a small group, with just one partner or working by themselves. In addition there are the other children they play with in school, and among them their close friends. In all this they need effective verbal and non-verbal skills. Communication through body language and other non-verbal signals develops naturally and underpins their learning. The spoken and written word and the structure of the language is unconsciously absorbed and used by the children in building their own language.

How the computer contributes to this process we shall illustrate by some examples. Gill Piper in her *Micromath* article 'Early years roaming' writes about her research with a class of 4–5-year-olds playing a game in which the Roamer took on the role of Postman Pat delivering letters to houses: 'The children cooperated well, with high motivation and constant discussion ... the activity helped to enhance their mathematical communication skills' (Piper 2001: 11). The article also describes the use of the Roamer with a Year 2 class with the aim of extending their work on measuring and estimating distances by using the Roamer as a non-standard unit of length for estimating and measuring:

> The class began with the children seated in a large circle around the teacher. It had been several weeks since they had last used Roamer so the first few minutes were a revision for the children on the use of the command-keys on Roamer's back ... The teacher then went on to ask who remembered how the Roamer travelled when FORWARD 1 was pressed. After some discussion, one child tried it, and all children agreed that 1 was the length of Roamer itself. There then followed a discussion on how many 'turtles' it would take for Roamer to move to H who was sitting at the far end of the circle from the teacher.
>
> (Piper 2001: 11)

The article goes on to describe the development of this work in which learning involved verbal/linguistic input and also the development of mathematical/logical and visual/spatial skills. In a subsequent lesson described in the same article one group decided to make the Roamer turn in a circle and one child did not understand what this meant until another got up and demonstrated it in action, an example of bodily/kinaesthetic learning. Other examples are counting on fingers and many computer learning games in which mathematical thinking involves coordination of hand, eye and brain, which contribute to the learning. Gill Piper includes some of the children's writing about what they liked and disliked about the Roamer – for example: 'I like the bit on roamer which is his butens becase [sic] they do good things and very good for making him go other ways'.

This is another case of children developing an understanding of mathematics through an activity in which they feel in control of the computer (in this case, Roamer) as they instruct it to do mathematical tasks.

Teaching the computer

In Chapter 5, Ronnie Goldstein and David Pratt discuss the value to children's development of having to understand a mathematical process in order to program a computer to carry out the intended steps to reach a planned outcome. Work with the Roamer enables very young children to engage in such learning activities.

When it comes to sitting in front of a computer, children sometimes work with a partner developing interpersonal learning. When they work alone the computer may seem like an extension of the child's own persona to facilitate intrapersonal and independent learning. Children themselves expressed their views about using computers for learning mathematics in a study carried out by the NRICH team in 2001 on the impact of the Internet on children's learning of mathematics:

> I find it easy to understand, I feel at one with the computer
> I can do it in my own time and on my computer its just generaaly [sic] easier.

In this study the children appeared to see the computer as a tool and another source for variety in learning that facilitates independent learning and provides opportunities for practice. In this relationship the computer is a private space, reflecting the child's own pace and learning needs, checking their work, giving immediate non-judgemental feedback and allowing them to try again until they get it right.

With handheld technology and a display screen or with the use of an electronic whiteboard there are many ways in which the whole class can work together. Here they learn from oral work, exploring mathematical ideas under the teacher's guidance. One system allows children to input their individual results from their handheld device to a central screen. Everyone has to give an answer and the class learns from discussing the mistakes made without identifying who made them.

The computer can become the assistant and friend of teachers and children. There is an increasing availability of dynamic support materials and e-learning activities for teachers to use in introducing and explaining mathematics and for independent study.

When children create their own animations to explain mathematical concepts, as in the case studies described by John Vincent in Chapter 4, they are also 'teaching the computer'. This is often with the objective of explaining the mathematics to younger pupils. Not only is the exercise highly motivating, but they also develop a deeper understanding and better memory retention of the related facts. In addition to the Logo-based MicroWorlds, programs such as Flash are being used by children to produce animated sequences illustrating mathematical concepts. For publication on web pages Flash has the advantage that the Flash reader is a free download and widely used (see http://www.tygh.co.uk/new.html).

The potential of the Internet to enhance learning

By opening up communications with the wider learning community, the Internet is radically changing schools by giving them free access not only to information sources richer than any school library but also to other schools, expert advice and reviews from other teachers about resources (see e.g. http://www.ictadvice.org.uk), and the opportunity to download and try out free software and free resources.

As an example of one use of ICT to enhance learning, the MOTIVATE project (http://motivate.maths.org), with the strapline 'You can be a mathematician' sets up videoconferences between primary classes in different parts of the UK, South Africa, India and Singapore and extends an open invitation to other schools to take part. Schoolchildren learn some mathematics that they would not normally meet in school; they work on their own practical mathematical projects; they give talks and presentations about their work; they share lessons from a university mathematician; and they communicate with pupils and teachers in other schools via videoconference links, web boards and email.

Teachers see involvement in MOTIVATE as a positive experience for their pupils and for themselves. In particular they identify the challenge such an experience gives their pupils, both to their mathematical thinking and in terms of the need to think about communicating their findings to other people. A Scottish teacher commented that, 'Some shine in new challenges'. A Newcastle teacher wrote, 'I feel you achieved your aim to provide students with the opportunity to do real maths, to be creative, to get away from single right answer problems and to enjoy working together on something completely different'.

In the evaluation of the first two years of the project, 57 per cent of the teachers said their perception of some pupils' ability to do maths had changed since their participation in the project. One London teacher commented that it was not always predictable who would be most enthusiastic, and it would not necessarily be those who were best at mathematics. The same teacher commented that she had revised her opinion of some of her students' ability after seeing them work on the problems, particularly some who were normally very quiet in class. Another London teacher commented on a girl who had not previously spoken in class at all if she could help it: 'She's been contributing in class, she's been putting her hand up . . . you know . . . it's just made her world a little bit bigger'.

The evaluation showed that teachers value the opportunity to widen their students' appreciation of what mathematics is about, and to give them the chance to use their skills in solving problems both within and beyond the normal curriculum, working in groups to bring about useful discussions. They also highlight the gains pupils experience by using technology effectively.

The Internet promotes a learning culture that is characteristically open and constructivist. We learn to use new software applications, (e.g. to build our own websites or to make PowerPoint presentations) not by expecting someone else to teach us step-by-step but by trying out the options from the program menus, observing what happens, looking for patterns and icons that suggest cause and effect, reading help files where we only partially understand the language and searching for meaning and reasons behind what we discover. Children are very good at this way of learning. In many families the children master the computer and the video before their parents. Schools should value and foster these learning skills and the Internet provides a very cost-effective learning environment in which to do so.

The future

Scientists in a Canadian laboratory have succeeded in making an atom act as an on-off switch which has the potential for miniaturizing computers to an atomic level. While the construction of a working computer the size of a pinhead is still on the borders of science fiction it is no more fantastic than present-day computers would have seemed not so long ago. It opens up the possibilities for creative applications of computers in science and medicine. In schools we cannot justify clinging on to teaching methods which emphasize skills and knowledge that may have been appropriate in the past but fail to prepare the children of today for their futures. If teachers find it a struggle to keep up with learning to use new technologies, that simply proves beyond doubt that educational methods of the past have not been particularly successful. The priority today is for students to learn to be efficient learners and creative thinkers.

Reference

Piper, G. (2001) Early years roaming, *Micromath*, 17(2): 10–13.

INDEX

ISSUES IN TEACHING NUMERACY IN PRIMARY SCHOOLS

Ian Thompson (Ed.)

This timely book provides a detailed and comprehensive overview of the teaching and learning of numeracy in primary schools. It will be particularly helpful to teachers, mathematics co-ordinators and numeracy consultants involved in the implementation of the National Numeracy Strategy. It presents an accessible guide to current British and Dutch research into numeracy teaching. Leading researchers describe their findings and discuss implications for practising teachers. The projects include studies of effective teachers of numeracy and ICT and numeracy, an evaluation of international primary textbooks, assessment, using and applying mathematics, and family numeracy. The book also includes chapters on pedagogy, focusing on the teaching of mental calculation; the transition from mental to written algorithms; the place of the empty number line; and the use of the calculator as a teaching aid. Most chapters include practical suggestions for helping teachers develop aspects of their numeracy teaching skills.

Contents

Section 1: Numeracy: issues past and present – Swings of the pendulum – Numeracy matters: contemporary policy issues in the teaching of mathematics – Realistic Mathematics Education in the Netherlands – The National Numeracy Project: 1996–99 – Section 2: Curriculum and research project issues – Primary school mathematics textbooks: an international comparison – Using and applying mathematics at Key Stage 1 – Family numeracy – It ain't (just) what you do: effective teachers of numeracy – ICT and numeracy in primary schools – Section 3: Assessment issues – Choosing a good test question – Context problems and assessment: ideas from the Netherlands – Section 4: Pedagogical issues – Getting your head around mental calculation – The empty number line as a new model – Written methods of calculation – Issues in teaching multiplication and division – The pedagogy of calculator use – Index.

224pp   0 335 20324 8 (Paperback)   0 335 20325 6 (Hardback)

NUMERACY AND BEYOND

Martin Hughes, Charles Desforges and Christine Mitchell with Clive Carré

One of the fundamental problems in education is that of applying skills and knowledge that learners have gained in one context to problems they encounter in another. This is particularly so in mathematics, where the problems encountered by learners in applying mathematical knowledge are well documented.

Using and applying mathematics has been a central component of the National Curriculum in mathematics. However, the National Numeracy Strategy has adopted a new approach, in which 'using and applying' is integrated throughout the mathematics curriculum. This book aims to help teachers develop their understanding and practice in this crucial area. It is based on the findings of a major research study, funded by the Nuffield Foundation, in which a group of primary teachers worked closely with the research team to develop their thinking and practice. The book provides a clear conceptual analysis of the problem of application, together with extensive examples of ways in which teachers can address it in their classrooms at Key Stages 1 and 2. A novel feature of the book is that it includes first-hand accounts of practice in Japanese classrooms, and outlines what teachers in the UK and elsewhere may learn from Japanese methods.

Contents
Introduction – The problem of application – Application in the mathematics curriculum – Teachers' ideas about application – Teaching for application at Key Stage 1 – Teaching for application at Key Stage 2 – Teaching for application in Japan – Application in theory and practice – References – Index.

136pp   0 335 20129 6 (Paperback)   0 335 21030 X (Hardback)